War, Memory, and the 1913 Gettysburg Reunion

War, Memory,

and the

1913 Gettysburg Reunion

Thomas R. Flagel

THE KENT STATE UNIVERSITY PRESS
Kent, Ohio

For the families of veterans

© 2019 by The Kent State University Press, Kent, Ohio 44242

ALL RIGHTS RESERVED

Library of Congress Catalog Number 2018052574

ISBN 978-1-60635-371-4 (cloth)

ISBN 978-1-60635-470-4 (paper)

Manufactured in the United States of America

LIBRARY OF CONGRESS CATALOGING-IN-PUBLICATION DATA

Names: Flagel, Thomas R., 1966- author.

Title: War, Memory, and the 1913 Gettysburg Reunion / Thomas R. Flagel.

Description: Kent, Ohio : The Kent State University Press, [2019] | Includes
     bibliographical references and index.

Identifiers: LCCN 2018052574 | ISBN 9781606353714 (cloth)

Subjects: LCSH: Gettysburg Reunion, 1913.

Classification: LCC E475.57 .F53 2019 | DDC 973.7/349--dc23

LC record available at https://lccn.loc.gov/2018052574

Contents

Acknowledgments

It takes a village to produce a monograph, and this work is no exception. Primary credit for this endeavor goes to my family and friends, who provided boundless motivation and support despite my continual absence. Great thanks also to Ken Allers Jr., for spending countless hours teaching me the phenomenon of Gettysburg. The work is based on a talk supported by Cindy Small and the Gettysburg Foundation, with research made possible with the help and expertise of the Tennessee State Library and Archives in Nashville, the Library of Congress staff and the National Archives, the John C. Hodges Library Special Collections staff at the University of Tennessee at Knoxville, Mike Sherbon and the Pennsylvania State Archives in Harrisburg, John Heiser and Tom Greaney of the Gettysburg National Military Park Library, the Adams County Historical Society in Gettysburg, the Wisconsin Historical Society at Madison, the Manuscript Division at the New York Historical Society Library, and many others. I am also eternally grateful to my many colleagues and students at Columbia State Community College who supported this work, especially Hoyt Gardner, Dr. Barry Gidcomb, Greg Mewbourn, and everyone at the Williamson County Campus.

Thanks to veterans John Sylva, James Beins, Charles W. Caldwell, Bill Radcliffe, and Ralph Walker for their insights concerning military tenure and memory. Critical to the editing process were Theresa Elworth, Will Underwood, Hazel Blumberg-McKee, Mary Young, and the staff at Kent State University Press; Michael Bryant of the US Department of Education; and novelist Ann Rushton.

Gratitude also goes to Jacki Sylva, Tim Pierce, Mike Skinner, Dr. Carol Codori, Barb Ross, Read Ridley, Drs. Rob and Laura Yost, Karl Green, and my publicist Barb Flagel for their support. Finally, innumerable thanks go to the many who have done their best to formally train me, including my professors at Loras College, Kansas State, Creighton, and Middle Tennessee State University, and for this project particularly Dr. Robert Hunt, Dr. Martha Norkunas, Dr. Mary Hoffschwelle, and Dr. Rebecca Conard.

Messiahs or Mortals?

June 16, 1913

Comrade:

Your name is on the list to go to Gettysburg. The trip will be by Providence Line boat, leaving Sunday evening, June 29. In order that there may be time to make complete arrangements you are requested to be at the boat, Fox Point Wharf, Providence, by 6 P.M. that day. An envelope will then be given you containing:

1. An individual round trip ticket, which you must sign; good until July 15.
2. A badge, which you are requested to wear at all times.
3. An identification tag, which you must fill in and carry in your pocket.
4. A pass, which you must show to gain admission to the camp. You should also carry your Discharge or a Certificate of Service from the State in which you enlisted, or Pension Certificate.
5. A bag tag. You are reminded that only hand baggage can be taken, each to handle his own.

When it became clear that the "Jubilee" Reunion of the Battle of Gettysburg was going to take place, after years of promising yet contentious planning, Rhode Island's commission chairman Elisha Hunt Rhodes and his officers sent the above circular to four hundred fortunate individuals within their jurisdiction. Months before, the committee members worried that few of their fellow residents would volunteer to go. Fearing a lack of interest, Rhodes issued more than two thousand printed invitations to every Civil War veteran organization in the state, beseeched newspaper editors to insert the announcement into their dailies, and sent flyers to postmasters in the remotest corners of the state. The response: more than six hundred answered in the affirmative.[1]

Surprised by the outpouring, Rhodes and his associates felt compelled to send a second message, trying to dissuade the surplus from attending. "Do you understand," read the notice, "you are to sleep in tents, and live on U.S. rations, cooked but issued as when you were in the Army. That you will be in these tents and live on these rations for at least four days, with no chance to hire a room or go to a hotel if you are sick." The commission gave each man one day to answer, and even then, over four hundred still said yes.[2]

The respondents would become part of the largest Union and Confederate reunion ever held. Over fifty-five thousand official attendees plus thousands more under their own volition descended upon a town of four thousand during the scorching summer of 1913, with the promise of little more than a cot and two blankets, military fare, and the presence of countless adversaries from a horrific war. Just to reach this site, some would travel nearly the length of the continent. Most of the men were revisiting a period in their personal history that involved acute physical and emotional trauma (the word *trauma* itself being the ancient Greek word for *wound*). All attendees lived in a country in which the average lifespan for a male at the time was fifty-one years, and their average age was seventy-two. The scenario raises a number of questions, not the least of which was, why did they go?

This is an exploration of that event and those individuals.

Contrary to popular belief, the prime motives for veterans to attend did not include national reconciliation, nor did the Great Reunion produce a general sense of a reunified country. The reconciliation premise, advanced by several major speeches at the anniversary as well as David Blight's influential *Race and Reunion: The Civil War in American Memory* (2001) and Stuart McConnell's *Glorious Contentment: The Grand Army of the Republic* (1992), lived in rhetoric more than in fact. More recent scholarship effectively dismantles this "Reconciliation of 1913" mythos, finding instead that sectionalism and lingering hostilities largely prevailed among veterans and civilians. Chief among these explorations are Edward Linenthal's *Sacred Ground: Americans and Their Battle-fields* (1993), John Neff's *Honoring the Civil War Dead: Commemoration and the Problem of Reconciliation* (2005), Robert Hunt's *The Good Men Who Won the War: Army of the Cumberland Veterans and Emancipation Memory* (2010), Barbara Gannon's *The Won Cause: Black and White Comradeship in the Grand Army of the Republic* (2011), Caroline Janney's seminal *Remembering the Civil War: Reunion and the Limits of Reconciliation* (2013), and Brian Matthew Jordan's *Marching Home: Union Veterans and Their Unending Civil War* (2014).[3]

While largely agreeing that sectionalism remained in place, *War, Memory, and the 1913 Gettysburg Reunion* differs from the preceding works by positing that, when veterans returned to a place of war memory, they almost invariably interpreted the site in personal rather than sectional or national terms. The phenomenon of shared experience often transcended a person's national, regional, and even regimental affiliations. Locations and events that may have become iconic in the collective civilian psyche, such as Little Round Top or Pickett's Charge, remained almost irrelevant to veterans who fought in other places. Time and again, veterans sought out others who endured the same specific circumstances they had, and the more precise the episode, the more intense the bonding that often followed. For the individual veteran in situ, national themes and narratives were at most tertiary considerations.

This study also finds that political declarations at the Great Reunion focused less on reconciliation and more on the praising of mass martyrdom. Repeatedly, high-ranking officials made celebratory references to blood, death, and salvation, and the overriding theme was messianic. For a country in 1913 on the precipice of becoming the world's most dominant international force, orators claimed a teleological revelation: Civil War veterans living and dead, especially those of Gettysburg, were the nation's saints and saviors, and the Reunion was to be their beatification. As Woodrow Wilson himself asserted on July 4, the last day of the commemoration, "we are made by these tragic, epic things to know what it costs to make a nation—the blood and sacrifice of multitudes of unknown men lifted to a great stature in the view of all generations by knowing no limit to their manly willingness to serve."[4]

Such verbiage followed standard social convention. Rooted deeply in Western culture was this assertion of collective unending life through human sacrifice. From Hellenistic and Roman praise for the selfless death in service to the whole to monotheistic principles of future salvation through past martyrdoms, the expression of devotion unto death demanded (and continues to demand) unwavering reverence.[5] From the highest officials in the Grand Army of the Republic (GAR) and the United Confederate Veterans (UCV), a score of state governors, and leading figures of the US House and Senate to the secretary of war and the commander in chief himself, a half century of reflection made it clear: being the bloodiest battle of the nation's bloodiest war, Gettysburg was not just a military engagement, it was the nation's Golgotha. The ransoms paid on its hills and plains were not only heroic, claimed the dignitaries, they were necessary. Perhaps William Appleman Williams best summarizes this enduring public mind-set: "In accordance with the logic and psychology of myth . . . it has become necessary to turn the [American Civil War] into something so different, strange, and mystic that it could have happened only to the chosen people."[6]

Did the veterans feel the same? Far less quoted and observed were the words and actions of the former soldiers themselves, save for a select few who spoke at formal events during the week. Public events like the Gettysburg Jubilee can easily overshadow the individual perspective. Part of the reason lies in the nebulous vocabulary involved. Words like *commemoration, celebration,* or *reunion* were—and are—easily interpreted as public rather than private experiences. The purpose of this study is to shed greater light on how individual veterans viewed the Reunion, what motivated them to attend, how they acted and reacted once they arrived, and whether these survivors found what they were seeking. This is in effect a case study of how survivors personally view themselves at such gatherings, regardless of what the official narrative might be.

My initiation into the particulars of the Grand Reunion occurred in 2013 as I prepared a lecture for the Gettysburg 150th Anniversary Commemoration at the National Battlefield Park. I discovered that six months of intense research barely scratched the surface of what happened in 1913. This brief volume is an attempt to further explore the views and experiences of those who attended that largest of all Civil War reunions. It is also one of many attempts to better understand a group to which I will likely never belong. My father, stepson, several other relatives, friends, and students are military veterans, a profession for which I am ill suited for many reasons but one that merits greater dialogue. Presently there are some twenty-one-million living veterans of the US military, many of whom are praised during major anniversaries and large public events with the same unctuous verbiage that President Wilson delivered at Gettysburg but are rarely allowed to speak for themselves in those same circumstances.

While we cannot converse directly with the long-passed attendees who tented by the tens of thousands at the Great Encampment, we can explore their photographs, newspaper interviews, letters and diaries, military records, regimental histories, marriages, friendships, and kinships.[7] The material herein involves accounts from many participants, but to further personalize the exploration, four attendees receive deeper consideration:

- Heman Allen of Burlington, Vermont, a veteran of the infantry at Gettysburg who later became a wealthy businessman and intensely patriotic.
- Moses Waldron, a working-class Virginian who survived Pickett's Charge, only to lose faith in the Confederacy late in the war.
- William Fickas, a Federal artillery gunner stationed on Cemetery Hill through most of the battle, who moved out west later in life.
- H. H. Hodges, an impoverished farmer from Appalachian North Carolina, who did not fight at Gettysburg but whose regiment did.

For this study, Allen, Waldron, Fickas, and Hodges were chosen because of the spectra they covered and their respective worldviews. Specifically, two fought for the Union and two for the Confederacy. Birthplaces included city, town, and countryside. Their regions of origin included the Northeast, Southeast, and Midwest. Formal education ranged from college to none. Two became officers while two remained privates. After the war, two stayed close to their home towns, and two followed the call to "go West." Professions included commerce, industry, service, and agriculture, and their income levels spanned relative opulence to bare subsistence.

As different as they were, the four possessed common traits. All were white adult males, born in the United States within five years of each other, had no military experience beforehand, were volunteers, saw extensive combat, and returned to civilian life immediately after the war. In addition, by 1913, all four were members of a rapidly dwindling minority—Civil War veterans who were still alive. Each in his own way found a different path back to Gettysburg, and each sought something unique once he reached his destination. Their departure differed as well. Among them, one would never manage to separate himself from his traumatic past, and one would not make it back home alive.

If there is a synopsis of the following, it comes from a statement made by a veteran, not of the Civil War but of a later and larger conflict. In the process of writing another work, I interviewed an individual who fought the Empire of Japan from the nose of a US Navy reconnaissance bomber. When asked how he viewed his experience in its entirety, Walter Joseph Bryant paused for a moment and said, "each man has his own war."

CHAPTER 1

Planning Glory

"We are approaching the fiftieth anniversary of the most decisive battle of the war for the suppression of the Rebellion. . . . It would be entirely in keeping with the patriotic spirit of the people of the Commonwealth to properly recognize and fittingly observe this anniversary."
—GOV. EDWIN STUART before the Pennsylvania
General Assembly, January 5, 1909

Born of an idea, the spectacle took longer to plan than the duration of the Civil War. Tradition credits Henry S. Huidekoper of the 150th Pennsylvania, who had lost an arm at Gettysburg, as the first to propose a grand commemoration. Fellow survivor John Page Nicholson, chairman of the Gettysburg Battlefield Park Commission, championed the concept. On the evening of September 8, 1908, Nicholson invited more than two dozen individuals to Gettysburg's Eagle Hotel and asked them to join the endeavor.

Within two weeks a second meeting at the Adams County Courthouse drew 150 people. The list of attendees read like a local geography primer; Donald McPherson (of McPherson's Ridge), William Ziegler (of Ziegler's Grove), Theodore McAllister (of McAllister's Mill), et al. gathered to see whether such an undertaking was even feasible. Heading the proceeding was the balding, bearded, studious president of the Lutheran Theological Seminary, Rev. Dr. J. A. Singmaster, who immediately downplayed notions that the celebration was a commercial enterprise. Although the thought of attracting an army of tourists certainly piqued the interest of merchants present, Singmaster instead established the official line going forward.[1] Building on the Old and New Testament foundations of redemption through human sacrifice, Singmaster reportedly insisted the Reunion "should be a celebration out of gratitude to Almighty God, who was on the side of the army most nearly on the right. It should be celebrated out of gratitude to the noble, heroic men who gave their lives here for a new baptism of liberty." Driving the premise further, he cited the voluminous bloodshed as evidence of Gettysburg's divine standing. "In the whole Revolutionary War," claimed the reverend, "only one-half the number of men fell in defense of the country as fell at Gettysburg." Seconding the sentiment, committee member Judge Swope added that Gettysburg was unquestionably "the greatest battle of the ages in bravery and results," which created "a united, prosperous, powerful nation, the common heritage of all."[2]

Blue and Gray reunions were nothing new. Postwar gatherings were initially few and far between, but the ensuing decades saw veterans congregate with increasing frequency and volume, sometimes with several thousand in attendance. One of the first formal joint reunions occurred in 1875 in Elizabeth, New Jersey. Atlanta held a modest affair in 1900. Gettysburg hosted similar events in July 1887 and in 1906, yet most combined events were at the division level.[3] The host community envisioned something far grander, in fact unprecedented, involving tens of thousands of former soldiers from both warring parties. In this pursuit, they offered a romanticized, battle-centric interpretation of the Civil War (a war in which most fatalities occurred from disease rather than combat) contested by heroic warriors for noble causes.

For such a veneration, Gettysburg seemed custom made. The battle was brief—approximately sixty hours. The engagement was thus free from the lurid stigmas of long sieges, like the protracted trials of Vicksburg or Petersburg. Nor did the campaign result in the innumerable complications of a long military occupation, as was the case in Chattanooga, Fredericksburg, Memphis, and New Orleans. For the martyrdom motif, it was the costliest battle of the country's deadliest war, a supreme *imitatio Christi*. "Gettysburg," wrote one commentator, was "a word made sacred by the river of blood that flowed from the wounds of thirty-six thousand of the world's best manhood."[4] The fight also had a rare quality; it suited Confederate and Federalist nationalists alike. Over time, Pickett's Charge had become the centerpiece of the Lost Cause narrative, in which a mighty host marched forth against (presumably) unbeatable odds and was driven back at enormous cost. Conversely, Unionist hardliners could also embrace this "watershed salvation of the North" as their greatest victory. As the *Nashville Banner* proclaimed in its coverage of the Reunion, "There was glory for both sides at Gettysburg."[5]

On a more practical note, the site also possessed logistical advantages. Convenient for an outdoor assembly, the town itself had not grown precipitously. While much of the country was undergoing rapid urbanization, Adams County was not. The passage of fifty years saw Gettysburg's population increase from twenty-five hundred to a little over four thousand, while urban sprawl was already enveloping the battlefields of Manassas, Fredericksburg, Richmond, and elsewhere. In addition, the federal government "owned" Gettysburg; the battlefield park had been under the direction of the US War Department since 1895. The town was also centrally located, a mere dozen miles from the Mason-Dixon, and within a day's journey from most coastal metropolitan areas.

Support accumulated quickly. By 1909 the Pennsylvania legislature authorized creation of a Gettysburg Anniversary Commission and appropriated seed money of $5,000. In June 1910, the US Congress formed a committee to coordinate with Harrisburg, prompting a first general summit in Washington later that same year. By 1911 Pennsylvania's assembly increased its financial support to $50,000 (over $1.2 million in 2018 dollars), and other state legislatures began to form their own bipartisan commissions.[6]

Many veterans also supported a 1913 pinnacle, as time was a factor. The US Pension Bureau calculated that roughly 2,880 veterans were dying every month, or one every fifteen minutes. In 1880, Kansas was home to some 145,000 war vets. By 1912 there were only 21,000 left. During a visit to the National Military Home in Leavenworth, the state GAR commander found 48 Gettysburg survivors. He estimated there were no more than 150 statewide, and of these, he hypothesized a third of them were too feeble to attempt the journey. In light of these declining numbers, Kansas announced that its statewide reunion scheduled for the spring of 1914 would be its last. In a similar survey, South Dakota officials discovered their state had only fifteen Gettysburg survivors. Rare were the weekly obituaries that did not mention the passing of another veteran. As Gov. George Hunt of Arizona admitted, "These old soldiers are not long for this world."[7]

The veterans themselves were of course intrinsically aware of their mortality. While leadership within the GAR and UCV touted the pending event's "permanent establishment of harmonious and fraternal relations between the North and the South," most of their members were simply trying to live a few more years. There is little evidence to suggest that survivors felt responsible, capable, or even willing to unify the nation's disparate regions, races, and factions. Concerning the Reunion, the most common question among them was whether they would be physically or financially able to go, or even if they would live long enough to see it.[8] Chances were better for the relative "youngsters" like Heman Allen and Moses Waldron, who would be in their late sixties when the anniversary transpired, while H. H. Hodges and William Fickas would be seventy and seventy-three, respectively. Even then, the aged were highly susceptible to cancer, dementia, diabetes, kidney diseases, pneumonia, stroke, tuberculosis, and most of all heart disease—the most prolific killer in the United States at that time.[9] Present, too, was the phenomenon of suicide among their contemporaries—more than 15 percent of suicides in the United States during the early twentieth century were people over the age of sixty. One among many was Charles W. Cook. In 1904 Cook checked himself into the Sawtelle, California, Disabled Veterans Home outside Los Angeles on the same day as William Fickas. Cook lasted only two years, killing himself in the facility after a long and debilitating illness. On the eve of Memorial Day 1911, Beacon Falls, Connecticut, resident Frederick Reffelt was dining with his family when he informed them that his grave would be decorated with blossoms, "with his comrades' graves, tomorrow." Reffelt then put a pistol to his head and pulled the trigger. In 1913, eighty-five-year-old Gavin Caukin of Portland, Oregon, also shot himself, "while standing in front of a cabinet filled with medals won in the service of his country." Two months before the Gettysburg Jubilee, a Chicago newspaper offered a short synopsis of one man's end: "Hiram Kennedy, Abington, Ill., civil war veteran, 70, suicide. Rope."

In many ways, death and loss infiltrated life and memory. Hodges's company lost twenty-four men even before the war was over, and his impoverished class suffered a high mortality rate thereafter. In peace-

time, Allen became a widower after just six years of marriage, and he
lost his second wife just before her sixtieth birthday in 1906. By 1913,
only five of Waldron's nine children were still alive. News of McKin-
ley's assassination reached William and Amelia Fickas mere hours after
the funeral of their own twenty-six-year-old daughter, the victim of a
gasoline fire. Accidents, injuries, and illness repeatedly presented life as
fleeting. Each year, tuberculosis alone killed more Americans than ten
Gettysburgs combined. Rather than glorify the past, most veterans were
privately trying to come to terms with the present and the growing pos-
sibility of being alone.[10]

In context, the Reunion became something to live for, a gathering at
which friends and fellow survivors would be waiting. This prospect wid-
ened considerably when in 1912 organizers announced that all honorably
discharged veterans were eligible to attend, not just those who fought
at Gettysburg. The expansion stemmed from the commission's desire
to create magnitude. Aside from the difficulty of determining who was
actually present at the battle, there was also the incentive to create a truly
national Civil War reunion. For men like H. H. Hodges, who joined his
regiment after the battle, and for veterans who never served in the Army
of the Potomac or the Army of Northern Virginia, the extended invitation was a welcome offer. Part of the attraction was the sheer enormity
of what was about to unfold. Six months out, the Williamsburg *Virginia
Gazette* predicted the Reunion would be "the greatest gathering of con-
queror and conquered in the history of the world." Slated to attend were
outgoing president William Howard Taft, chief justice Edward White,
Speaker of the House Champ Clark, and the newly elected Woodrow Wilson.[11] Gettysburg itself was becoming a tourist destination. Construction
of its massive cyclorama was well under way, new park roads were being
laid by the mile, and Congress was considering the construction of a Lincoln Memorial Highway from the nation's capital to the world-famous
"turning point" of the American Civil War. The only major obstacle left
involved paying for the thing.[12]

Like the war itself, its Jubilee was going to be expensive. The largest
cost involved transportation. For the tenant farmer in Hodges, attendance
would require the purchase of a train ticket, a daunting proposition for
a man with almost no property to his name. The round-trip price for his
departure point of Mount Airy, North Carolina, to Gettysburg would be

$11.65 (equivalent to approximately $286 in 2018). Moses Waldron, still working as a night watchman at sixty-nine, would have a much higher bill from his home in remote Carthage, Missouri, a community just a few miles from the Kansas and Oklahoma borders. William Fickas advantageously lived near the major rail hub of Phoenix, though his ticket price would still be seven times that of Hodges's. Many veterans faced similar circumstances, living too far from family and/or financial independence to travel by their own means. The situation prompted a call for legislative action, exemplified by a January 1913 editorial from the *Bismarck Tribune* pleading, "the great majority of the old soldiers of North Dakota are men in very moderate circumstances. Could not the state well afford, as a matter of sentiment and of patriotism, to appropriate a certain sum of money which should go toward defraying the expenses of all of the old soldiers to the reunion that is to be held at Gettysburg next July?"[13]

In past instances, reunions were most accessible to men like Heman Allen—from the upper classes and high-ranking officials in veterans' organizations. This was especially the case for Allen, a well-to-do man whose portfolio read like a ledger of the Industrial Revolution. Recently retired from the mercantile trade, Allen owned a business and his own home on Burlington, Vermont's Main Street, a sizable policy with New York Life, and multiple savings accounts. His stocks and bonds included investments in railway companies, including the powerhouse Pennsylvania Rail Road, as well as Pacific Power and Light, an emerging communications concern named American Telephone & Telegraph, international titans American Sugar and United Cigar, People's Gas, Andrew Carnegie's behemoth U.S. Steel, and cold hard cash invested in the Baldwin Refrigerator Company. For most others, such wealth was inconceivable.[14]

Complicating the matter was the already contentious Pension. By 1913, assistance to Union veterans and their dependents cost the US Treasury some $150 million per annum, and the weeklong commemoration at Gettysburg was projected to cost an additional $150 million in federal spending. An editorial in the Salt Lake City *Goodwin's Weekly* warned of the growing prowar grandiloquence and the rush to the public coffers. "A man can't throw a stone into any crowd without hitting a hero," it observed, adding that to shower all veterans with adoration was a dubious exercise at best, regardless if the year were 1863 or 1913. "Men who wore the blue and men who wore the gray will mingle together in peace, if they get someone else to pay their bills. . . . They did well their work—some of them. Some of them didn't, by the way. . . . The plain nineteen hundred and thirteen truth is that the old soldiers have demanded too much." As the *Topeka Daily Capital* put it, "we doubt that the plan to send Kansas survivors of the battle to the Gettysburg reunion will arouse much interest. One reason is that it will cost money to do it. The others are unimportant."[15]

Many voices also questioned whether it was prudent to fund a celebration that would feature secessionist flags and uniforms. Others wondered if Northern states should financially support the hundreds of former Confederates living within their borders (for example, over 10 percent of veterans residing in Indiana had served in gray). As David Blight finds, some of the most adamant skeptics were African American newspapers, which openly asked why veterans of the Confederacy merited considerable amounts of public assistance while black citizens toiled under the apartheid polity of Jim Crow.[16] Per *Goodwin's Weekly*'s acerbic comment that "the old soldiers have demanded too much," the argument may have carried weight in the late nineteenth century. Yet by 1913 the dwindling number of veterans was not the sizable voting demographic it had once been. Further, while veterans' organizations showed great interest in the Reunion, the driving forces, especially when it came to funding, were younger politicians.

Presented with an opportunity to appeal to the patriotic voter base, and to democratize access to the national event, legislatures from every state that remained loyal to the Union allocated public funds for transport to and from the Jubilee. Allen's Vermont provided $10,000 (or about $245,000 in 2018 dollars). Fickas's birth state of Indiana set aside $20,000 for its residents, state commission, and official guests. Waldron's adopted Missouri allotted $15,000. Most other Northern legislatures offered similar amounts. Unmatched were the assemblies of New York and Pennsylvania, which labored to outbid each other in their ongoing rivalry for prominence upon the nation's most renowned battlefield.[17]

For decades the Empire and Keystone States maneuvered and manufactured their way to top billing on the Gettysburg marquee, mostly by physically marking their territory. New Yorkers eventually installed a tablet, marker, or memorial for every single one of their infantry regiments, cavalry troops, and artillery batteries present at the fight. One of the largest reunions the field had yet seen involved the dedication of the New York State Monument in 1893.[18] For the upcoming semicentennial, New York budgeted $265,000 to send twenty-five thousand of its soldier-citizens. Voicing concerns of overcrowding (and fearing they would be overshadowed on their own political turf), the Pennsylvania Commission capped New York's attendance to ten thousand and later reduced it further to eighty-five thousand. In turn, the Pennsylvania legislature ballooned its own contributions to nearly $500,000. Amused by the bidding war, the New Orleans *Times-Democrat* quipped, "Americans dearly love a big national demonstration of this kind."[19]

The pressure to present a patriotic air certainly extended to Washington, DC. Along with funding, feeding, and sheltering the Reunion, Congress also moved to appropriate monies for veterans living in the district to receive free rail passage to and from Gettysburg. On the first ballot, the tally was almost undisputed, the lone dissenter being the Twelfth District of Texas's Rep. Oscar Callaway. To boast unanimity for the $4,000 bill, his colleagues deftly lured the fiscally and legally prudent Callaway out of chambers and rushed a revote in his short absence. The duped lawmaker returned frustrated and embarrassed, but he was able to laugh at the successful ruse.[20]

Characteristic of the American political tradition, officials who might have agreed on the necessity of patriotism could in turn possess wildly different visions on what patriotism entailed. In late January 1913, the Gettysburg Commission assembled in Philadelphia to finalize major components of the anniversary. Present were heads of the UCV and GAR, federal government liaisons, leading citizens from Gettysburg, and individuals representing twenty-one states. On paper, all looked in good order. Beneath the semblance of building excitement, anxieties persisted. Looking to create a sense of unity at the event, Col. Charles Burrows of New Jersey proposed that no uniforms or flags be present. The flying of Confederate flags especially, Burrows reasoned, would not foster an inviting atmosphere to Union veterans who had successfully yet laboriously managed to remove the banner from Pennsylvania fifty years previous. Several Southern delegates rejected the proposal outright, none more emphatically than Col. Felix H. Robertson of Texas, the same Colonel Robertson implicated in the killing of unarmed African American troops during the Saltville Massacre of 1864. Between expletives, a clearly agitated Robertson insisted that the Reunion should not present itself as an assembly of civilians, nor should the setting be entirely neutral:[21]

> There was never a greater mistake in the history of the world than the Civil War; but, on the other hand, you veterans of the Grand Army of the Republic have never made peace, and the credit for the feeling now existing between the people of the North and the South is due to your sons and not to any of you. We only quit fighting when we were forced to, speaking for myself, we would have been fighting yet if we had not seen that it was a hopeless task to defeat you. We were forced into the Union, and now we ask that you take us as we are. Allow the old Confederates to go to Gettysburg in their tattered uniforms. Many of them do not know that the war is over. . . . The feeling down South is that we should all come back for the last time wearing our old uniforms and carrying our muskets, cartridge belts and tattered flags.[22]

The assertions sparked heated reactions. Those with Northern ties questioned the validity of Robertson's demands, and chairman Louis Wagner openly chastised Robertson for his incendiary language.[23] A series of disturbing revelations worsened the situation. Several men were shocked to hear, only five months before the anniversary, that multiple legislatures were not going to subsidize travel for their veterans. Gettysburg Town Council member Dr. Singmaster admitted that the host village had no available funds either, to which Wagner openly voiced his growing belief that Gettysburg was "neither patriotic nor progressive enough to sacrifice a little to make the celebration a success." Others openly questioned whether a town of four thousand could accommodate the expected tens of thousands of non-veterans who were also coming to the event, because neither Pennsylvania nor the War Department were making any plans to address that side of the equation. The night's meeting—taking place at the Union League in the City of Brotherly Love—had done much to debunk the prevailing rhetoric that the martyrdom of thousands brought everlasting peace.[24]

Fearing his landmark festival was falling apart, Pennsylvania governor John Tener moved to calm the troubled waters. Standing as tall as Lincoln at 6'4", the clean-shaven, Irish-born Tener calmly proposed a kind of personal sovereignty: the individual soldier should decide what he brings. The politically progressive Tener couched his amendment in language both conciliatory to Confederate sentimentalists and congratulatory to their Unionist counterparts. He referred to all Southerners as "welcomed guests" of Pennsylvania and the Union army. The terminology soothed and dignified former secessionists (including the marginally reconstructed Robertson) and yet painted his state and its 1863 defenders as victorious and magnanimous hosts. After much wrangling, Tener's offer won the day.[25]

Despite its cleverly worded diplomacy, the enigmatic phrasing quietly magnified a lingering disconnect: the most vehement Confederate nationalists were beginning to see themselves and their doctrine as legitimized and accepted in the eyes of their adversaries, while in fact Tener's wording depicted Southern veterans as de facto visitors to their own nation. This temporary fix also failed to rectify the problem of marginal support from legislatures located in the former Confederacy. While maintaining a tradition of "states' rights" arguments, Southern statesmen refused to financially support the men who fought for secession. Of the original seven Confederate states, only South Carolina's state government appropriated funding, using an amalgam of revenues and notes to cobble together slightly over $3,000. Alabama offered nothing, nor did the assemblies of Florida, Georgia, Louisiana, and Mississippi, nor Colonel Robertson's Texas. By comparison, Iowa's legislature budgeted $10,000 (despite having no regiments at Gettysburg), Michigan provided $20,000, and Minnesota $25,000.[26]

Notwithstanding the posturing and pandering at the state level, when it came to loyalties, veterans occasionally spoke fondly of their home state, but their behavior gravitated toward the practical. In search of employment, support bases, or other opportunities, they often migrated. Heman Allen still lived in his birth state of Vermont, but many of his comrades moved far away after the war. Hoosier-born William Fickas moved back and forth between Arizona and California. Of those making the trip from Fickas's old home of Indiana, their legation consisted of men who fought for eleven Union states, four Confederate states, and the US Army Regulars. After the war, Virginian Moses Waldron paradoxically returned to southern Pennsylvania in search of work. In September 1865 he returned briefly to his home state, left again for Pennsyl-

Federal attendees predominantly opted for civilian attire, whereas former Confederates commonly appeared in gray uniforms supplied by their respective United Confederate Veterans chapters and support groups. A few on both sides wore their original uniforms. (Courtesy National Photo Company Collection, Library of Congress)

vania, moved to Indiana after seven years, and finally settled in western Missouri.[27] In the larger context, H. H. Hodges was the exception rather than the rule, living in the same county in which he was born.[28]

When state funds were not forthcoming, veterans often took the initiative to find their own way. GAR and UCV chapters raised funds for their members. In late June 1913, a movie house in High Point, North Carolina, dedicated the proceeds of a night's showings to help raise money. Others made the trek by their own means, often with friends and family.[29] Newspapers played major roles. Former Federal William Fickas and ex-Confederate J. J. Camp joined forces with Phoenix's *Arizona Republic* to solicit contributions. The newspaper itself printed a payment slip that readers could send in along with cash. Gen. George W. Stone, a key figure in organizing Michigan's pilgrimage, appointed Michigan's *Lansing State Journal* to receive donations in addition to what the state had already provided, adding, "if the newspapers do not interest the public in the matter, the whole trip may have to be abandoned." Such a forfeiture was quite possible in places like Texas, where the *Houston Post* and other newspapers were the central clearinghouses for travel money. Said one man, "if the *Post* had not taken it up, we would not have gotten there."[30]

Philanthropic though they were, such endeavors often revealed old animosities. In the North and the South, certain circles felt that any veteran wishing to attend should receive material support, provided he served under a specific side. Behold the generous *Houston Post*. Seeking private donations, it asked contributors to vote for the former *Confederate* they wanted to send, even though former Union soldiers lived in and near the city as well. Those who received the most votes would have their transportation covered.[31] Houston's American Brewing Association gave conditionally, formally stating, "our reason for contributing to this fund was purely sentimental. All of us here are Southerners, and, of course, we have a warm place in our hearts for those brave men who nobly fought for the Southland in the dark days of the early '60s."[32]

Others looked to foster a martial presence of the Old South in the northern venue, including Mississippi United Daughters of the Confederacy member Lucy Green. She pleaded for her state to send as many men as possible who had served under Robert E. Lee, whom she praised as "the mightiest man in the tide of time." The UDC of Pulaski, Virginia, held a fund-raiser "to uniform those indigent Confederates who want to go to the Gettysburg reunion." Pleased that some one hundred men from UCV Camp A. P. Hill were planning to attend, the Richmond *Times Dispatch* said, "the members of the camp will go in uniform and carry their flag," adding that the group was "one of the best drilled veteran organizations in the South, and expects to make a fine showing." With tactical wording, the *Arkansas Democrat* looked forward to covering the event where "the *men* who fought under the stars and stripes mingle with the *heroes* of the stars and bars" [italics added]. Among many of the Confederate veterans, their incentive to attend was usually less defiant. When asked why he signed up to go, F. R. Jones of Houston said, "I had not had a chance for a vacation in years and years."[33]

Still, willingness to participate depended on the individual, and each had his own reasons. Long before the Jubilee, Heman Allen organized and attended smaller reunions regularly. Born in 1844 in Westford, Ver-

Confederate Veteran Coupon
TRIP TO GETTYSBURG

I vote for..

for the trip to Gettysburg. He was a Confederate soldier and a

member of.. regiment.

He is a citizen of Harris County.

.... Voter.

This coupon must be clipped from a copy of The Houston Post
and must be received in the office of The Post before 8 p. m.
Thursday, June 26, 1913, to be counted. If received after 8 p. m.
it will not be counted.

Pages of the *Houston Post* featured donation forms, including the ballot (*left*) to nominate a specific Confederate veteran to attend. As with most Southern state assemblies, the Texas legislature did not provide travel funds for its residents, leaving companies, private citizens, and the *Post* to raise the money on their own. (*Houston Post*, Houston, TX, June 26, 1913)

mont, Heman grew into a studious and organized young man. He prospered in Vermont's exceptional public school system, and in his teens he became a clerk in a county store (his first step into a lifelong journey of commerce). At age eighteen, during the war's second year, he joined Company A of the 13th Vermont Infantry, where his skills in mathematics and writing landed him the job of company clerk. The role would lead him to be the company's de facto historian.[34]

Allen was fortunate that much of his service was clerical; he was not inclined to violence. By nature sentimental and loyal to those near him, in 1864 Heman was intent on reenlisting, but his mother pleaded that he return home. Being her only child, he obliged. Like most of the war's survivors, Allen tried to readjust back into civilian life, yet the goal proved elusive. Building a career as a dry goods merchant, he became materially successful over time, but he still missed the comradeship of his younger years. In 1888 he played a central role in forming the 13th Vermont's first regimental reunion. By the turn of the century he had become a full-fledged, flag-waving patriot, a leading officer in his local GAR, active in the Sons of the American Revolution, and a member of the Society of Colonial Wars.[35]

By 1913 Allen was retired and living with his son and a live-in maid at his upper-middle-class home in Burlington. He was so well regarded as an organizer and veterans' advocate that he was invited to the Union League Building in Philadelphia to be a part of the Gettysburg Reunion Commission. There, Allen, Elijah Hunt Rhodes, and others began to finalize plans for the Jubilee.[36]

In contrast, Virginian Moses Waldron had become almost utterly disconnected from his wartime past. Like many fellow veterans, he wished to forget as much of the conflict as possible. Born in Roanoke and with an adolescence that would be neither scholastic nor secure, he held little affection for his formative years, including his time in uniform. In his middle teens Waldron labored on a farm with his younger brother, assisting an older relative on a hardscrabble plot in Bedford County. He was only seventeen when he joined the 28th Virginia in 1861, mostly on the assumption that the war would be a brief and preferable break from his monotonous and unremarkable life. From there Waldron's time in the Confederate Army eroded him. Repeatedly sick or wounded, he weathered the war from First Manassas onward. At Gettysburg, he was in the epicenter of Pickett's Charge, marching into the Angle with a cousin, several close friends, and an uncle, losing most of them in the process and barely escaping alive himself.[37] By the start of 1865, the treadmill of engagements had killed or maimed most of his regiment. By April Waldron was in Washington, DC, officially listed by the provost marshall as a refugee and "rebel deserter." In September 1865 he married his hometown sweetheart Fannie Clingenpell, and they eventually moved to Carthage, Missouri, where there were no members of his old outfit anywhere near him.[38]

On the eve of the Reunion, Waldron was neither poor nor wealthy. By all indications he was reasonably grounded. Despite a hard life that left him in chronic pain and stoop shouldered, he was able to work as a night watchman. Fannie and he were still together and had welcomed several grandchildren into the world. He was amiable, outgoing, and modest yet sociable. When the chance to return to Gettysburg emerged, thanks in part to available funding from the state of Missouri and an invitation from an old comrade, he decided the "celebration" was at least worth a look. Still, he viewed his upcoming journey with trepidation, mostly because he did not know what he would find.[39]

Drifting in between the nostalgic and detached were the likes of former Hoosier William Fickas and the lifelong Virginian H. H. Hodges. Fickas saw much of Gettysburg from his Union artillery battery stationed on Cemetery Hill, and he felt compelled to see the place again. Born in Indiana in 1841, Fickas eventually apprenticed as a barrel maker and was living with his extended family when the war began. He joined the 14th Indiana in the summer of 1861. Blue-eyed and with sandy hair, Fickas was somewhat diminutive at 5'5". He nonetheless rose in rank higher

Clean-shaven Heman Allen stands (*front and center:* person no. 5) among the commissioners of the Third General Conference for the planning of the Reunion. In the second row (*second from the left*) is Elijah Hunt Rhodes of Rhode Island. Perhaps intentionally, the unreconstructed Felix Robertson of Texas and UCV official C. Irvine Walker distance themselves in the first row to the right. (*Fiftieth Anniversary of the Battle of Gettysburg: Report of the Pennsylvania Commission*)

than most. After seeing combat in the Shenandoah with the 14th Indiana, he transferred to the 4th US Artillery in June 1862, with which he would serve through the Gettysburg campaign and beyond. Discharged at his end of service on April 19, 1864, Fickas reenlisted into the 143rd Indiana as a first lieutenant, later earning a captaincy.[40]

Later in life Fickas worked as an engineer and raised a son and daughter with his wife Amelia. Despite attaining a degree of wealth, he had never returned to Gettysburg before the Reunion and was only marginally connected with veterans' affairs. But the promise of revisiting the increasingly famous battlefield influenced him to bring as many nearby veterans of any stripe along with him as he could.[41]

Then there was Hodges of Surry County. Born in 1843 on the leeward edge of Appalachia, he was likely christened Hubbard, the same name as his father. Yet documentation throughout his life presented a myriad of iterations—Hubard, Hubert, Hubart, Herbert, Henry. His muster sheet of April 1864 offers a clue as to why. Private Hodges signed the document with an X. Later census reports would confirm that, from cradle to grave, Hodges could not read or write.[42]

Like many who ventured to the Gettysburg Reunion, Hodges did not fight in the battle, but in his case he had an incentive to connect with those who did. The regiment he joined in 1864 was the 21st North Carolina, a unit that suffered 28 percent casualties in the battle, mostly when it tried in vain to dislodge Union infantry and artillery from Cemetery Hill. Hodges's late entry into the war stemmed from being the oldest child of four still at home, his older brother James volunteering for the Confederate Army soon after North Carolina's secession. While his own future regiment marched into Pennsylvania, Hodges remained in the service of his family and added to it when he married his sweetheart Martha in June 1863. Except for his stint with his regiment, Hodges and Martha would remain together for the rest of their lives. Theirs was an existence of hard times, never once owning the ground upon which they toiled. The pair moved several times, always within a few dozen miles of his birthplace, trying to make each rented, marginal plot produce more than the last. Although he lived near many fellow Confederate survivors, there is no record of his being involved in veterans' activities until the Jubilee. He listed himself as disabled in the 1880 Census, although by necessity he continued to farm his lease, struggling along with his neighbors in one of the poorest counties in the state. In 1913 he decided to travel to a place that had grown exponentially in the American mind but was a site unseen to him.[43]

CHAPTER 2

Getting There

"Today fifty thousand veterans of the Great War are moving on to take peaceful possession of the field where in the ardor of youth they strove in such deadly conflict."

—*NEW YORK HERALD,* June 28, 1913

After a veterans' state commission approved his application to attend, he received a package in the mail containing his badges, identification tags, a camp pass, and a label for his one allowed bag. For Allen, Fickas, Hodges, Waldron, and most of the recipients, also in the envelope was a round-trip train ticket. The nation's sprawling rail network was a major reason why the Reunion reached such unprecedented size. During the war, there were some 30,000 miles of rails in operation, a revolutionary amount albeit positioned mostly in the North and almost exclusively east of the Mississippi. By the time of the anniversary, the United States hosted over 250,000 miles of iron, enough parallel track to reach the moon. These were the avenues upon which the majority would conduct their pilgrimage.[1]

Over seventy separate companies were involved, including more than forty in Pennsylvania alone, some of which were familiar to the men who rode them during the war, such as the Baltimore & Ohio (upon which Lincoln traveled to and from Gettysburg for his oft-quoted visit) and the Memphis & Charleston (a prize that spawned the Battle of Shiloh).[2] Other entities were born from the postwar boom of the Industrial Revolution. The 160 veterans departing from Seattle were leaving on the Great

Northern, a contiguous line younger than most of their grandchildren and impressively swift. A century before, the expedition of Lewis and Clark needed fifteen months to travel from the banks of the Missouri to the shores of the Pacific. The Washington delegation made the return trip from Seattle to Omaha in about three days. Most of North Dakota's 165 representatives made it from Fargo to Gettysburg in a little over two days. H. H. Hodges and his companions traversed the four hundred miles from his local station of Mount Airy, North Carolina, to the commemoration in about fifteen hours.[3]

In many instances, the send-off itself was cause for celebration. When two Union and nineteen Confederate veterans gathered at the Rice Hotel in Houston, Texas, they were treated to a serenade of sorts when representatives from six different rail companies pitched their respective routes and perquisites. By a narrow vote, the Southern Pacific and the Louisville & Nashville split the victory, after which the party retired to the Post Building for a celebratory group photo. Over two hundred people from the small community of Belvidere, Illinois, escorted their three representatives to the local train depot and the wartime creation of the Union Pacific Railroad, with a fife and drum corps leading the way. Grander still was Minnesota's valediction, with forty-seven members of the 1st Minnesota et al. receiving badges and flowers at the Minneapolis courthouse, followed by a festive banquet in the veterans' honor at the Commercial Club, and then a parade down 3rd Avenue led by a drum corps. The send-off at Detroit's Central Depot verged on the monumental. A massive assembly of family, friends, aid societies, and fellow veterans bade good-bye to six hundred Michigan men. Bands played, onlookers cheered and cried, and the Daughters of the GAR pinned blossoms to the lapels of the departing.[4]

It was a Wednesday evening, June 25, when Fickas and his companions stepped into a car of the Atchison, Topeka, and Santa Fe. Waving them good-bye were a crowd of supporters, journalists, and officials, with their populist governor George Hunt personally offering wishes of good health and safe travels. Joining them was the amiable William G. Hartranft, a state-appointed chaperone tasked with making the entire excursion as enjoyable as possible.[5] Ahead of them lay a trek of twenty-five hundred miles. The first leg involved a brief stop in Ash Fork, at 2:40 A.M. By sunrise they were in Winslow, where the party grew considerably larger as it joined an incoming train of fellow veterans from Pasadena.

Upon reaching Albuquerque, the entire entourage climbed aboard a special "No. 4 Veteran's Train" with the sun setting to their backs. From then on the group made excellent time, reaching Kansas City by Friday and the end of the Atchison, Topeka, and Santa Fe in Chicago's Dearborn Station by Saturday morning. Lunch and a brief jaunt over to Union Station had them on their way aboard the Erie Line, the Western Maryland RR, and to the Gettysburg depot on Sunday afternoon with a day to spare.[6]

For Heman Allen and several hundred Vermonters, their six-hundred-mile trek began on a serene, cloudless morning. Among them was Frank Kenfield, a colleague of Allen's from the 13th Vermont. He recalled, "as the train moved on, all seemed joyous and happy. One would be led to think as he listened to their jokes and laughter, they were boys instead of men that had passed the allotted time of human life."[7]

Anticipation had been building across the country for some time, sustained by wishful thinking among many that the Reunion could act as a domestic elixir or at least a temporary diversion. The United States of 1913 was hardly a placid entity: severe racial unrest, cyclical nativism, extremes in wealth and poverty, urban overcrowding, and the threat of war in Europe. For some, 1863 seemed almost worthy of nostalgia by comparison, a perceived age of faultless heroes and ennobled struggle. Looking back, the Philadelphia *Evening Telegraph* waxed, "the days of the Civil War now belong to the historian, the poet, the writer of romance and the dramatist. That period has enriched American history beyond computation."[8]

Less acknowledged were voices like that of an older woman seen standing just beyond the crowds at the Detroit station. A reporter approached her and inquired why she was distancing herself from the festivities. "I saw a train just like this start for Pennsylvania in '62," she reportedly said, "it was grand and awful sad—when the boys went away. But they didn't all come back. War is an awful thing, sir."[9] A minority of editorials offered similar caveats, few more directly than the Charleston *News and Courier*:

> Do not let it come to pass that this Great Reunion on the bloodiest field of the great war shall tend to glorify and exalt war itself. Let us, on the other hand, realize, if we can, the horror of those three days. Let us picture, if we can, the carnage at the Bloody Angle. Let us feel, if we can, the grief that settled down upon thousands of hearts in the North and in the South

when the lists of the dead were published in the newspapers. At Gettysburg men butchered one another. At Gettysburg thousands died in agony.
Let us try to see the thing as it was—to see it in its crimson horror and all
its ghastly cruelty. . . . If only the whole world could succeed in seeing it as
it was, another Gettysburg would be impossible.[10]

Symbolizing a cautious approach to the anniversary, some veterans
journeyed to Gettysburg in small numbers and almost unnoticed. As
Moses Waldron prepared to leave Carthage, he was looking for a single
person. When asked if he had any comrades traveling with him, Waldron responded, "One, and the only one I know of." Hoping not to go
alone, he wrote to his former lieutenant, William J. Gooley, then residing two hundred miles to the northeast in Callaway County. The two had
not seen each other in forty-three years, but a series of letters led to a
promise to meet at the grand St. Louis depot and leave together. The two
believed themselves the only surviving members of their company, and
their reuniting almost didn't happen. Upon reaching the river city, Waldron wandered for hours, looking in vain. Finally he came upon his old
officer, admitting, "When I found him I did not recognize him." When
the two approached each other, Waldron simply said, "Comrade," and
shook Gooley's hand.[11]

Waldron's need for companionship was understandable. This was not
a journey to be taken lightly. Vastly improved engineering and a number of enforced federal regulations made train travel far safer than it
had been during the war, but the massive machines were still capable of
breaking bodies at random. Just two years before, Waldron's own daughter was killed in a railroad accident, a loss that continued to haunt him.
Then there were the factors of age and health. Waldron suffered from
curvature of the spine. The US Pension Bureau listed Heman Allen as
an invalid. William Fickas lived with rheumatoid arthritis and heart disease. Hodges had endemic heart problems. For many of the larger cara-
vans, sponsors took the extra precaution of sending chaperones, doctors,
and nurses along.[12]

As they all made their way to their national rallying point, another
danger surfaced: a punishing national heat wave. Waldron and Gooley
experienced temperatures above 100 degrees in St. Louis, while others
struggled in the upper 90s around Indianapolis, Louisville, Richmond,

and Washington. The dangers, especially to the very young and old, were beyond mere discomfort. A week before the anniversary, towns in northern Michigan and Wisconsin saw fatalities from sunstroke. Chicago suffered more than forty heat-related deaths over the week, including twenty-nine in a single day. In late June, dehydration and other complications claimed an estimated sixty infants in the city of Cleveland alone.[13] Pennsylvania wilted too. Families in Pittsburgh attempted to evade their radiating buildings and streets by sleeping in city parks at night, and they still lost more than a score of people, including eight deaths in a twenty-four-hour period. As a consequence, some veterans begged off, unable or unwilling to take the risk.[14]

Still, most of the veterans came, in part because of the adventurous journey itself. This was an opportunity to see new places and old friends along the way. Departing from Houston, Levi Hickey stepped aboard the International & Great Northern to see his old hometown in Kentucky. Nebraskan Andrew Bush and his granddaughter stopped to see relatives in Brazil, Indiana, before heading on to the Reunion. Texan J. D. Townshend thoroughly enjoyed his time on a more southerly route. "We were treated royally from the time we left Houston," Townshend recalled. "I was particularly impressed with Montgomery, Alabama, which is the best lighted city I ever saw." A member of the 5th Wisconsin, John Blundell, augmented his journey to the east with a stop at his sister Mary's home in Wilmington, Delaware. The siblings last saw each other in 1863, when he was recovering in a Chester, Pennsylvania, hospital from wounds he received at Gettysburg. Devout Mormon J. W. Reed tied in a visit to the Atlantic Ocean (which he had never before seen), with a visit to his brother in Port Byron, New York, and a sojourn to the former home of Brigham Young.[15]

All made the trek acutely aware the trip alone could be arduous and the destination involved living for days in a tent city with primitive accommodations. What they likely did not know was how thoroughly the US Quartermaster Department prepared for almost every contingency, including the probability that at least some would die during their stay. With that in mind, the quartermasters built a temporary morgue inside the camp itself, contracted embalmers, and shipped in a carload stacked full with more than fifty empty caskets.[16] To be certain, this was an era in which life was routinely dangerous. Many wanted to go but never made it. Seventy-year-old William Groescup was training his temporary replacement at his coal trestle job near Rochester, New York, when he lost his footing alongside the coal conveyer, fell into the whirling machinery, and was crushed to death. Washington Hands, a station agent in New Orleans, made it all the way to his sister's home in Maryland, where he became ill and died. Francis Kells was set to leave his home in Brooklyn when his appendix began to pain him. He went into the hospital for surgery and died from complications.[17]

Due to financial constraints, many states and philanthropists placed a cap on representatives; for instance, Utah promised to fund only sixty-five attendees. Altogether, sixteen state and territorial legislatures offered no financial support whatsoever. In the case of Myerstown, Pennsylvania, situated near the city of Reading and its eponymous railroad, and only ninety miles distant, the city counted at least forty-seven living residents who fought in the war, virtually all of whom were eligible for funding from the state. Still, ten were unable to go, primarily because of poor health, including one who had been wounded at Gettysburg.[18]

For those who could not make it, some communities simply made their own reunions. On June 29, veterans met in Chicago's Englewood Baptist Church to hold a midwestern Gettysburg commemoration. In Oakland, California, some five hundred gathered for an anniversary picnic and celebration. Citizens of Portland, Oregon, organized a dinner for those who had to stay behind. Ninety-three veterans gathered in a suburb of London, England, to commemorate the battle's anniversary.[19]

For the main event, the country vicariously shared in the buildup. Even clerics caught "Gettysburg fever." On the eve of the Reunion, a pastor addressed his Sunday congregation in Poughkeepsie, New York, and spoke of the example about to unfold to their west. He told his parishioners, "it is without doubt one of the most exceptional and unique events in history." For members of the Salt Lake City Immanuel Baptist Church, their service featured the sermon, "God's Guidance at the Battle." Reverend Bowerman insisted the topic was especially fitting, since their own deacon, Norman D. Corser, was not only a Gettysburg survivor, the former private of the 5th New Hampshire was on his way to the site at that very moment. The meaning of the battle, Bowerman added, had become self-evident to the country and the world: "Gettysburg is recognized as the crisis of the great civil war." He added that the reason for the engagement's outcome had also become clear over time. "As the years pass and the perspective grows better, men are seeing that the time for the turning of the great contest had come. Men are admitting that God was ruling." "That day," proselytized the reverend, "saved the nation." Other messengers heralded the concurring themes of martyrdom and messianic salvation. The *Baltimore Sun* called Gettysburg an "altar of patriotic sacrifice."[20]

Salvation aside, some men were most insistent on reaching the event, regardless of the obstacles. Eighty-five-year-old John Hawley feared that his son wanted to keep him from going, so the elder Hawley crawled out a window and caught a train to the commemoration. Former lieutenant W. H. Wright gave himself plenty of time, starting his journey from his Winchester, Virginia, home on June 9. He arrived seventeen days later with nearly a week to spare, having walked the eighty miles through the Appalachians on his own.[21] Reportedly, a federal counterpart named Peter Guibert also walked to the Reunion, traversing the two hundred miles from Pittsburgh to Gettysburg in three weeks.[22]

If one were inclined to trek with less effort, disposable income was most efficacious. For a small fee, veterans taking the steamer from Providence, Rhode Island, could enjoy the privacy of one of its two hundred staterooms on board or sleep on one of a hundred mattresses flopped onto an open space for free. Once they reached Pier 15 on New York's North River, a special breakfast awaited, for 50 cents.[23]

Better still, some drove in at their leisure, many upon Ford's increasingly accessible Model T. To make the last miles amenable, the state of Pennsylvania oiled the roads outside of Gettysburg for twenty-five miles in nearly every direction, and the state supreme court intervened so that all tollhouses from Chambersburg and Petersburg lifted their many gates, enabling road warriors to reach the event uncharged.[24] For these motorists, there was still the nuisance of traffic jams once they neared their destination. As one Hoosier observed at the city limits, "All of these roads are jammed and packed black with automobiles, with wagons, [and] with buggies."[25]

The resulting festive atmosphere may have been more compelling for Union veterans, who enjoyed a dominant position on several levels. Coming to a Northern state and place of Union victory, the numbers were also overwhelmingly in their favor. For every Confederate who made it, there were seven Union men present. The imbalance played out in microcosm on the weeklong train ride from Seattle. Veterans from each warring party crowded into the eleven cars for their momentous journey. "There are both 'Johnnies' and 'Yanks' on the train," said a man who had served with the 123rd New York, "but nothing but friendly feeling prevails." His comrades felt in the position to be cordial. "Besides, there are only eight 'Johnnies' and there are about 150 'Yanks,' so you see they would not stand any more chance against us now than they did 50 years ago."[26]

For H. H. Hodges and others traversing the South and up along the Atlantic Seaboard, the trip may have produced mixed emotions, because many of the routes passed through towns and sites eponymous with death and destruction. A common path for North Carolinians passed through the Virginia town of Orange County Courthouse, Lee's point of origin in the costly Battle of the Wilderness. From there they moved through Brandy Station, Manassas, and past Arlington.[27] Fellow North Carolinian J. T. B. Hoover took a slightly different route, but the travails were the same. "The trip took us through some of the great battlefields, Fredericksburg and around Richmond, and some of the breastworks have not yet been leveled. They seem to stand as silent sentinels, marking the awful tragedies of this war."[28]

The destination likely did little to assuage reservations. In many respects, white Southerners were venturing into unfamiliar territory. Dr. W. B. Prather from Seale, Alabama, marveled at the lush, tall crops of wheat and corn, and the equally bewildering sight of "no colored people working in the fields."[29] In preparation, Southern higher-ups encouraged ex-Confederates to present something of a united front. When Hodges received his pamphlet in the mail on how to prepare for the trip, the instructions were much like the ones received by his Federal counterparts, with a few select edits. Whoever read the brochure to him would have mentioned how all entertainment, food, and lodging were free. He was told to bring his own soap and towel, given instructions on how to send and receive mail while encamped, and was informed that the camp would officially open on June 29. Yet North Carolina's UCV officials inserted an addendum: "veterans will as far as possible wear the U.C.V. uniforms and carry their camp flags. Confederate battle flags which waved at Gettysburg in 1863 could be carried with great propriety." Hodges, like most of his companions, consequently decided to wear gray.[30]

Once Hodges neared the commemoration, he may have even felt the sensation of being watched, because he was. New York correspondent Lindsay Denison noted how "all along the railroad one sees women standing at the doors of their homes in their yards staring at the trainloads of soldiers. Whole families living at a distance from the railroad took their lunches and picnicked on the embankments." Arriving at Gettysburg, many Confederates expressed a degree of cautious optimism, while others opted to wait and see. For the first hours after arrival, observed Denison, Confederate veterans had "as yet shown but little enthusiasm."[31]

Aside from their own corner of the camp, most Tar Heels knew there was at least one other sanctuary for them, thanks to C. H. McConnell of Chicago. McConnell was once an officer in the Iron Brigade, a unit virtually incapacitated for the remainder of the war after suffering devastating losses on Gettysburg's first day. In a letter to the North Carolina delegation, he warmly wrote, "I will erect upon the grounds of the reunion a headquarters tent for the Iron Brigade and as special guests Pettigrew's North Carolina Brigade. It will have a seating capacity of 1,200 canvas benches (easy to sit for the old boys), a stage and proscenium on which will be given some sort of entertainment every afternoon and evening. . . . Our headquarters will, of course, be headquarters for all the North Carolina representatives, irrespective of what brigade they served with, and all Confederates will be heartily welcome."[32] Despite the distance and heat, each passing mile contributed to a building anxiety in strange lockstep with a youthful excitement. Trying to corral a herd of old men to their connecting trains, a porter in New York sighed, "they are like a lot of boys." Said an enthusiastic veteran marveling at the bustling interior of Grand Central Station, "we're all younger than when we started away."[33]

CHAPTER 3

Arrival

"This second Gettysburg is a greater triumph than the first."
—*BALTIMORE SUN*, June 29, 1913

Quartermaster James Normoyle, directing operations on the ground, estimated there would be around five thousand to six thousand arriving by June 29—two days before the start of formal events. He and his associates were taken aback when the first wave exceeded eighteen thousand. Normoyle and company scrambled to accommodate the surge. With impressive zeal, the War Department responded quickly to calls for more blankets, mattresses, and food. In terms of public relations, this was a good problem. Scores of reporters on-site sent streams of excited telegrams describing the deluge.[1]

Also caught off guard, for different reasons, was journalist George A. Campsey. "It was a sad sight to see many of the veterans carried from their trains," wrote Campsey. "Some were minus limbs, others had lost arms, many were shy eyes or ears." Another writer attested, "there was a pathos in the eagerness with which the old men rushed to reunions, but the pathos became heart-rending when the spectators saw the slender little groups that formed the old regiments." Fellow reporter Lindsay Denison said the first arrivals appeared "feeble and uncertain of themselves."[2] Denison added, "Just now a white-bearded man, tottering with a flat-topped, faded blue hat bearing the crossed insignia . . . passed the *Evening World* tent. He seemed eighty years old. He was leaning heavily on a khaki-cladded boy with his arm across the lad's shoulder and his claw-like fingers clutching nervously at the youngster's sleeve. They are a sad, worn lot as they come in, these old soldiers; they are tired. . . . They march through the tented streets shuffling silently to the shelter assigned for them."[3]

Among the first "walking wounded" to arrive was William Fickas, possibly favoring the leg that had taken a Confederate bullet during his Shenandoah campaign. Arriving on later trains, Heman Allen looked relatively young with his clean-shaven face and tailored attire, but H. H. Hodges and Moses Waldron certainly counted themselves among the impaired. Waldron was shot at Malvern Hill, Hodges at Plymouth, Virginia. For most veterans, injury was part of their being, a normalcy, though some bodies possessed more visible damage than others. Among those with crutches or canes were Maryland native Charles W. Stuart, minus a leg from the Battle of the Wilderness, and E. M. Gibson, one of the commissioners from California, who underwent a lower limb amputation at Gettysburg. John Moody of the 24th Michigan Infantry had no lower right arm. Harry Simmons of St. Louis made his way on a wheelchair, having lost both legs at the Battle of Cold Harbor. Meeting each other for the very first time on June 29 were Henry Huidekoper and Elisha Wise, the former a survivor from the 150th Pennsylvania and the latter from the 11th Pennsylvania. Encountering each other on Seminary Ridge, they immediately recognized a shared trait; each was missing a right arm. An ensuing conversation revealed that both received their wounds within minutes of each other and only a few hundred yards apart just north of that same ridge.[4]

The most famous amputee to arrive was the extrovert extraordinaire Gen. Daniel Sickles. Once again embroiled in scandal (this time involving a fortune in missing funds from a monument account), Sickles was almost always surrounded by press. He basked in the attention and still claimed to have saved the Union on Gettysburg's second day. Yet being the last of the corps commanders still alive from either side, even the eccentric Sickles knew his limitations. The legend would stay outside of the Great Camp as a guest at the Rogers House, not far from where he famously lost his leg in the fight in front of Cemetery Ridge. Despite his celebrity, Sickles held marginal interest for the veterans who did not serve directly under him. They were more interested in their own pursuits.[5]

The most consistent destination for these early arrivals was to venture straight from their trains to where they stood a half century earlier. Frail and failing Hugh Meller of Fairport, New York, was determined to see the room where he had been held captive for two days. With the help of two other men, the seventy-four-year-old Meller struggled up a flight of stairs to the second story of the Western Maryland Railroad Station. "All these later years I have feared that the old station had been demolished," Meller told a reporter, "so you may know how glad I was when I saw the familiar building upon my arrival." Confederate F. O. Yates wanted to see precisely where he clashed with Union infantry on July 3. "I charged within 50 feet of the Federal lines on top of Gettysburg Heights. I will see if I can find the exact spot where I was struck with a Federal 'minnie' ball that caused me to remain in the hospital until the war was nearly over. . . . I presume that it has changed considerably since I participated in Pickett's Charge, but the same old hills will be there, and the same old rocks." F. M. Easton came in hopes of occupying the same room in the Eagle Hotel that he did on June 30, 1863, while on reconnaissance. Evidently he "almost wept" when he found that someone else had reserved the room. The occupant, seeing how much reliving the moment meant to Easton, doubled with another resident and allowed Easton to fulfill the wish.[6]

A North Carolinian marveled at their energy: "they took in the sights with a vigor that was remarkable, considering the age of the veterans and the fact that many of them had just completed long and tiresome journeys." Despite positive signs, some like journalist Campsey wondered if the event was too arduous: the long journey, the heat wave, and army life. One of the more famous arrivals synopsized the general veteran position. John Francis Key, grandson of Francis Scott Key and formerly of the 1st Maryland of the Confederacy, "came into town, weak and almost dropping," noted a reporter. Still, Key would not be deterred, asserting he was "going to see Gettysburg on this occasion or die."[7]

Fears among the public nonetheless persisted, especially with the news that men were dying almost immediately. One did so upon arrival. A former member of the 1st Maine Cavalry, Augustus Brown entered his assigned tent and lay down. Soon after, tent mates found him unresponsive and called for an ambulance. He died on the way to a field hospital. Moments later came an emergency call from the New York section. John H. Reynolds of Port Chester made it to the hospital before succumbing. Witnesses said he arrived at the camp exhausted, ate dinner, returned to his tent to reminisce with his roommates, and fell over. Papers on his per-

The importance of place. (Courtesy Harris and Ewing Collection, Library of Congress)

son listed his wife as his emergency contact. Several more women would become widows during the Reunion. The only question was how many.[8]

In the weeks leading up to the commemoration, officials suspected that the turnout could exceed their estimations. Dangerous shortages of food and shelter could result. When informed that the number coming would almost certainly top fifty thousand and not the forty thousand previously expected, secretary of war Lindley Garrison told the Gettysburg Commission that he would "not be responsible" for the overflow.[9] Notably, officials on the scene did not share Garrison's negative view. Col. James Schoonmaker, head of the Gettysburg Commission, saw the long lines of railcars, packed roads, and growing multitudes as wonderful, "more stupendous than we ever dreamed of." Their guests almost universally concurred. In several cases, the first response was one of pleasant surprise.[10]

Each veteran came armed with a formal invitation that read more like a summons, much like the one that Rhode Island veterans received in the mail. "Are you going to Gettysburg?" the note quipped. "When you arrive you must carry your own baggage to the Camp, and you are to sleep in tents, and live on U.S. Army rations."[11] The dire invite may have read almost like a ruse to some when they first rolled into town. Rather than seeing a boot camp, what they encountered was more like a vibrant, bustling, albeit well-organized carnival. A New York columnist observed: "On the skirts of the camp ground and in the village itself there is the air of a circus day. Clustering close up to the limits of the camp are the gaudy posters of the showmen, telling of the marvelous feats of the beasts that 'eat 'em alive' or of the titanic size of the fat ladies. In the village itself thousands of sightseers are quartered. Every room that is available was taken days ago, and the veteran without credentials and the civilian who had not enough foresight to make arrangements are sleeping in any bed that they could find."[12]

Journalist Charles Gillespie informed his readers: "Imagine the biggest street carnival you ever saw, then multiply it by a thousand. Recall the excitement of the midway, with its barkers, shops and side shows, picture a combination of dozens and dozens of lawn fetes all going full blast at the same time, and you have some idea of what Gettysburg looks like from center to circumference. Every street is blazing with flags and pendant buntings, almost every house has been transformed into a gaily decked 'hotel.' Every side yard and lawn is fitted up with alluringly pretty booths and refreshment stands."[13]

Contributing to the festive air, citizens garlanded the town square in red, white, and blue. To accommodate families, tourists, and the media, Philadelphia entrepreneurs rented open land just north of the National Cemetery. Upon ten acres wedged between Taneytown Road and Baltimore Pike they fashioned a small tent city and dubbed it "Meadeboro," complete with running water, privies, and its own field kitchens. The campsite could hold up to two thousand people. The enclave became home to "Newspaper Row" with some 150 correspondents, employees from Western Union, twenty photographers hopping hither and thither, and a humming web of telegraph wires overhead. Tenting among the pressmen and sutlers, other civilians filled in the remainder of available cots at $1.50 a night or $6 for the week.[14]

Inside and outside Meadeboro bustled a testament to the growing culture of American consumerism, brought to the public by a small army of merchants selling food, print, and souvenirs. There were dinner plates with "Pickett's Charge" painted upon them, conch shells bedecked with

While organizers and elites dictated the speech making, journalists and photographers connected with the veterans, gathered their stories, and recorded
their experiences. (Courtesy Pennsylvania Historical and Museum Commission,
Pennsylvania State Archives, RG 25.24, Records of Special Commissions, Fiftieth Anniversary of the Battle of Gettysburg)

scenes of the battle, hat bands, buttons, illustrated books, fresh fruits,
maps, and newspapers. One onlooker believed there were enough coun-
terfeit bullets, sabers, and swords for sale to "fill the Chesapeake Bay."[15]
As the *Baltimore Sun* reported, "to be entirely au fait one must live in a
tent, buy souvenirs and wear a uniform. Everybody's doin' it."[16] Working alongside the hive, columnist George Campsey informed his readers back in Pittsburgh, "on all sides is the souvenir man, the cane man,
the medicine man, the postcard and novelty man, the peanut and circus
lemonade vendor and the 'hot dog' man."[17]

Despite warnings that "no provision for civilians, nor means of getting about the vast field of battle, have been provided by the government or the commission," most of the arrivals simply walked the mile
from their trains to their tents. For veterans with the inclination and the
cash (and some states provided a few dollars for spending money), there
were herds of buggies, wagons, and automobiles ready for hire.[18] Also

at their service were 385 lads from the recently created Boy Scouts of America, handpicked from Philadelphia, the District of Columbia, and other nearby municipalities, bedecked in their new uniforms and eager to carry a bag.[19] "Just a motion or a call," remarked veteran Walker Blake, "and one was immediately at your side, ready to wait on you, or run an errand or do anything else to assist."[20] Capt. John Delaney added, "those splendid boys were in evidence everywhere." The young men reminded Delaney of his own troops during the war. So many in his company were barely older than these helpful teens.[21]

Making their way southward, at some point near Cemetery Hill the men exited Gettysburg proper and beheld an engineering marvel, a sprawling encampment of five thousand brand-new tents lined up in precise and numbered rows, a "brown city" constructed in less than three months. The appropriately named Great Camp was a massive polygon a mile wide by nearly two miles long, stretching from the southern edge of town to a point near the Codori farm. When Hodges began his journey to reach this place, his point of departure was Mount Airy, the largest town in Surry County, with 3,900 residents. The Great Camp had already exceeded that number by the morning of June 28. Sometime around noon of that day the camp's population surpassed that of Waldron's Carthage with its 9,000 townspeople. By midnight it was larger than William Fickas's Phoenix of 18,000. On the morning of June 29, it surpassed Heman Allen's Burlington, by far the most populous city in Vermont, with 21,000 citizens. At its height, the tented city would outpopulate all their hometowns combined.

In form and function, the complex was not a throwback to the war but a monument to the modern age of progressivism, and the veterans overwhelmingly expressed gratitude for it. Instead of being a biohazard (as many wartime encampments were), this rapidly constructed virtual city was efficient, orderly, safe, and clean. Within the camp, organizers had laid down forty-nine streets stretching west to east, with the Gettysburg & Harrisburg Railroad bisecting the entire enterprise north to south. Every street was numbered in sequence, as was every tent (leading some veterans to forget which number was which), a precise grid totaling more than forty-seven miles of roads. Hodges would have been directed to 35th Street West, the heart of the North Carolina section on the camp's western side. On his way Hodges passed the sixty-five

Train-weary veterans walk the mile from the station to their assigned camp locations, most toting the one small bag of personal items they were allowed to bring with them. (Courtesy George Grantham Bain Collection, Library of Congress)

tents set aside for Allen's Vermont men, positioned in one of the prime shady spots along the tree-lined Confederate Avenue. Ten states later he reached the appointed section for North Carolina, an area among the largest of the Confederate representatives, second only to Virginia. Hodges's next-door neighbors to the south were Moses Waldron, William Gooley, and the Missouri assembly. A half mile east, William Fickas and the Arizonians found their needle in a haystack, two shelters on 33rd Street East, surrounded by the sections for California, Delaware, Illinois, and New Hampshire.[22]

The gateway to each locale was the state headquarters, little more than an awning slightly larger than the occupancy tents, often decorated with flags and banners. North Carolina's accoutrement may have been a great benefit to Hodges in his search for home turf. Their standard featured the image of a giant foot, hard to miss, especially with its black tar heel waving in the breeze. But then came time to register, a difficulty for individuals like Hodges. During the war, somewhere between 5 to 10 percent of white adults in the North could not read or write, and for Southern whites the ratio neared 20 percent. In some rural counties of North Carolina, it reached 40 percent. For Hodges, his wife, their eldest daughter, and for many in his hinterland community, illiteracy remained a lifelong challenge. Walter Blake of New Jersey encountered a Southerner in a similar predicament as he was signing in, "an old boy in grey nudged my arm. 'Comrade, you'll put my name down for me, will you?'"[23]

After registering, Hodges then received his tent number. From there he started down the rows, walking along the maze of support ropes and open flaps. Upon reaching his assigned shelter, Hodges poked his head in and saw an arrangement of eight canvas and pine rod cots. Draped upon each were two army blankets, superfluous in the heat of the day but barely adequate for the cool night to come. On top of those sat a mess kit—his to keep—consisting of a knife, fork, tablespoon, teaspoon, a 1.5-pint tin cup, and a tin plate. Along the base of the wall were a pair of ceramic washbasins and a galvanized iron bucket for all housekeeping needs, plus two lanterns to help navigate the night. Hodges may have been able to decipher a paper note attached to a post that brought welcome news, "Information for veterans, Meals will be served as follows: Breakfast from 6.30 to 8.00 A.M. Dinner from 12.00 to 1.30 P.M. Supper from 5.30 to 7.00 P.M."[24]

Readily apparent was the sweltering heat trapped under the canvas. A high sun, sopping humidity, and temperatures nearing 100°F made the prospect of a sound nap elusive, so he may have ditched his travel bag and headed for cool groves and company along Seminary Ridge. As one observer noted, "Thus far the veterans already here have contented themselves very largely with sitting about in shady places talking."[25]

As for Hodges's appearance in military attire, Union counterparts apparently found it to be a novelty rather than a statement of Southern nationalism. Vermonter Joseph Stone casually observed, "nearly all of them wore their old grey uniforms." Another Union veteran joked, the Confederates "came in their gray uniforms, and were a fine-looking, well-preserved lot of old men. We must admit that the 'Johnnies' would have taken the first prize over we 'Yanks' had the function been a beauty show rather than a reunion."[26]

Seen as equally beautiful, if not more so, were the multiple features of modernity. An unexpected perk for Hodges and all veterans was the plethora of water fountains dotting the street sides, a luxury unfathom-

State headquarters for North Carolina on the west side of the Great Camp.
(Courtesy National Photo Company Collection, Library of Congress)

able in wartime. Constructed weeks in advance, sprouting from four ar-
tesian wells, spreading out across the encampment through underground
pipes and chilled as they passed through ice-packed coils, soothing gallons of cool spring water offered a welcome respite to the dehydrated.[27]
The encampment's fountains might have tasted particularly sweet to
those who remembered the sweltering summer of the Gettysburg campaign. Throughout, both sides struggled to find clean water. The battle
itself made many feel as if they were in a desert. Under a climbing sun on
July 2, the 15th Alabama marched some twenty miles (much of them with
dry canteens) just to get to the base of Little Round Top before launch-
ing their many charges against the famed 20th Maine. For Heman Allen
and his comrades in the 13th Vermont, their thirst was so severe that they
later carved the memory into their monument along Cemetery Ridge:
"haste was so urgent that an order forbade leaving the ranks for water."[28]

Memories of serving in heavy wool and living under thick canvas in
summertime also crept into the minds of many as they walked about
their new accommodations. More than one visitor described this khaki
tent as "a furnace," but nearly as many were grateful that the structures

A veteran shoulders his US War Department–issued cot, either in search of a shady napping spot or better roommates. (Courtesy Harris and Ewing Collection, Library of Congress)

were brand new. There were also the drinking fountains; field kitchens with their coffee, milk, and tea; the official camp commissary selling ice cream and soda pop; various vendors selling iced drinks; and the hotels and taverns with their Pilsner beers on tap and well drinks at the ready, indulging the men who were told to expect much less.[29]

As for the threat of Spartan rations, the first dinner on June 29 consisted of fresh-baked sweet potatoes, bread and butter, coffee, ice tea, roast beef, string beans, and vegetable soup, followed by ice cream and cakes.[30] If anyone missed the dinner bell, vendors, cafes, and taverns in town readily fed the surplus. As one partaker phrased it: "Stands line the streets of the town. . . . ice cream cone makers, sandwich makers, hot dog makers and purveyors of Pennsylvania's purest pie. There is hardly a doorstep in Gettysburg not occupied by someone selling lemonade or some other cool stuff. . . . Ice cream cone boys and the native fried chicken manufacturers, all ready to stuff a veteran until the ambulance comes, if he has but the price. Pickett's Charge is not to be compared with the charge of refreshments in Gettysburg today."[31]

As a safeguard, the government subjected all hawkers to certification and inspection for the duration. Worried that the combination of summer heat and feasting on delicacies would create widespread intestinal problems, Pennsylvania Commissioner of Health Dr. Samuel Dixon warned the encampment against partaking in too many "soft drinks." So pervasive were doubts within the medical community concerning the effects of soda consumption that there was an ongoing court case between the US government and the Coca-Cola Company involving the product's contents. State agents of the Dairy and Pure Food Department also tested the integrity of ice cream samples via lab work at Gettysburg College and consequently shut down several ice cream salesmen because their wares did not have a required amount of butter fat. Reportedly officials closed multiple orangeade and lemonade stands because the contents hardly contained any citrus, and according to a Washington reporter, tasted "worse than wood alcohol."[32]

There were benefits to all this fastidious regulation. By coming to the Reunion, veterans soon learned they were entering a healthier place than most of them had left, and far better than the world of the 1860s. Armed with a myriad of progressivist weapons—advancements in germ theory, improvements in disease prevention, the 1906 Pure Food and Drug Act, the 1906 Meat Inspection Act—the federal government and the State of Pennsylvania waged a fierce battle against sickness at the anniversary, and won. The Reunion was also the first ever field assignment for the National Medical Reserve, and its first order of business involved thoroughly inspecting the health of camp staff. Before being allowed to work, all two thousand food handlers underwent physical examinations on-site. Hundreds of cooks, bakers, and assistants were deemed a health risk and were summarily dismissed. Those who passed, their certificates in hand, filed into the quartermaster's tent to receive their respective assignments.[33]

Very little was left to chance. To preserve perishables, organizers brought refrigerated railcars to the battlefield. Temporary latrines, positioned at the end of each camp street and away from water sources, underwent ample applications of disinfectants, and laborers burned contents every night. Regular Army personnel visited each of the five thousand veterans' tents every morning to ask if anyone was sick or needed help. An Indiana visitor believed it was as if "the United States army was taught a lesson by the Spanish war, when lack of proper sanitary precautions and unpreparedness in other ways, cost the government

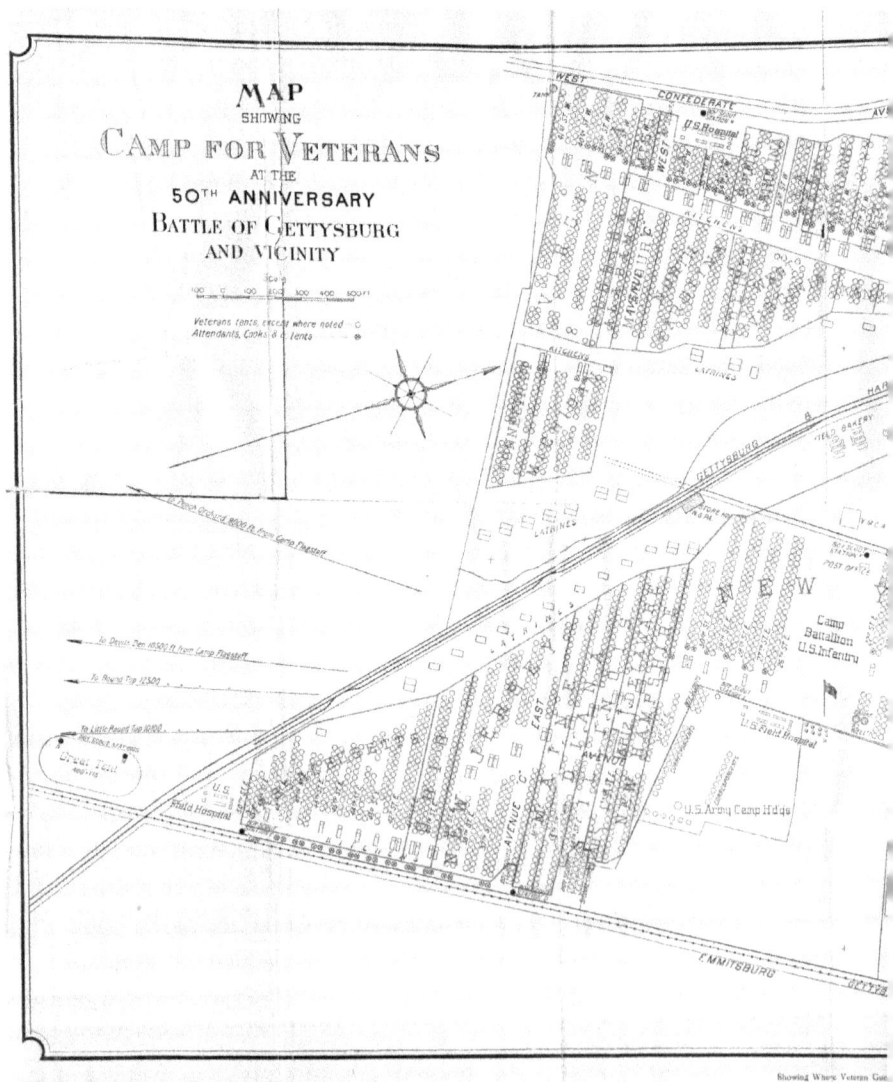

Map of the Gettysburg Encampment. (*Fiftieth Anniversary of the Battle of Gettysburg: Report of the Pennsylvania Commission*)

the lives of more men than were sacrificed to the bullets of the Span-
iard."[34] There was good cause to recall the 1898 conflict. As volunteers
fought in Cuba and the Philippines, the US War Department shipped
tons of canned meat to them, much of it treated with dyes and chemi-
cals to mask various stages of the contents' degradation. Thousands of

ts of Each State Were Located in Great Camp.

servicemen became gravely ill and an unknown number died, prompting whistle-blowers like Gen. Nelson A. Miles to chastise his own government for such gross negligence. Miles himself was scheduled to be
one of the celebrity attendees at Gettysburg, but duty pulled him to a
monthlong mission in the Balkans, where he was to monitor the region's
growing volatility.[35]

Back in the States, with the eyes of the nation upon Gettysburg, government officials (especially the War Department) dared not repeat the
scenes of their previous military expeditions. Should any facilities offend
the senses, or an episode of food poisoning erupt, or worse (for example,
the death of any veterans from negligence), there were scores of journalists, hundreds of cameras, and thousands of tourists and attendees to
spread the facts like a plague. It was one thing to promote public duty
among the youth, to send them into harm's way in a foreign place in the
patriotic pursuit of freedom and democracy. Losses in crusades were almost expected; indeed, at events like the Reunion they were exalted. But
to lose a frail and cherished savior of the nation from federal incompe-
tence or poor planning could be a very different narrative altogether.

Such caution and care naturally appealed to the veterans, who saw
innumerable friends and strangers succumb to food- and waterborne ill-
nesses during their war. Typhoid, for example, killed at least ten men in
Hodges's company. In Heman Allen's regiment, the disease sickened and
killed from their mustering in Vermont onward, and many of his colleagues remained carriers for years. The malady was still a viable killer in
1913. Moses Waldron's old comrades in Richmond, Virginia, weathered
a citywide typhoid scare just days before the anniversary, and a similar
outbreak erupted in West Reading, Pennsylvania, during the Reunion
itself. But public demand, and administrative action, helped lessen the
threat that had previously plagued entire legions.[36]

The war's most prolific ailments, dysentery and diarrhea, were almost
nonexistent at the Reunion. Thankfully so. Intestinal sicknesses nearly
incapacitated William Fickas's 14th Indiana during the Shenandoah Valley campaign. As if the Battle of Gettysburg were not lethal enough, the
Army of the Potomac recorded 5,890 cases of "the fluxes" in July 1863;
Waldron's Army of Northern Virginia fared as badly; and the following year, a punishing bout of dysentery sent H. H. Hodges to the infir-
mary and eventually knocked him out of the war.[37] Revisiting Gettys-

burg proved to be a far more positive experience for veterans' digestive systems because of tremendous regulatory work conducted behind the scenes. More than a year before the Jubilee, commissioners mandated the inspection, treatment, and monitoring of all water sources in the Gettysburg area, no small task considering that the Marsh Creek watershed in which the town resided covered over fifty-seven square miles. A dozen Health Department officials visited every property in the valley and discovered that nearly a third were contaminating the groundwater via seeping cesspools, manure piles, pigsties, and privies. In addition, one-third of all wells, cisterns, and springs were found to contain traces of raw sewage. Similar conditions likely existed in 1863, but by 1913 concordant advances in scientific process and public health advocacy enabled resolutions. Every hazardous source was either placarded with warning signs, securely covered, and/or permanently closed.[38]

To provide fresh water for 100,000 visitors through an infrastructure that supplied fewer than 5,000, Pennsylvania's commissioner of health assumed temporary control over the Gettysburg Water Company. For a week, technicians cleaned and tested all filters and pumps. For field hospitals and aid stations, engineers tapped into the city's main lines. In case of emergency, the commissioner decided to retrofit gasoline-powered engines on three of the town's four wind-driven water wells and assigned workers to man them "day and night" for the duration of the encampment. By the time veterans and tourists arrived, the town could safely supply a million gallons every day.[39]

Should the heat or any other eventuality prove excessive, organizers spared no effort in establishing a well-organized network of care facilities. Anticipating difficulties, chief surgeon A. E. Bradley mandated the main support system of eleven hundred beds, a 24/7 ambulance corps (mule wagon and automobile), emergency supplies, and an interconnecting communications system. On location were the American Red Cross, the US Army Medical Corps, the Medical Reserve Corps, and the Pennsylvania Health Department. Nearly every state was encamped within sight of one of the five large field hospitals plus eleven aid stations within the tent city itself. Augmenting these were an additional fourteen Red Cross stations positioned at the major tourist destinations throughout the battlefield park (the Virginia Monument, Little Round Top, Devil's Den, etc.). In direct contact by phone were the city hospitals

More than any other resource, the Gettysburg Commission and the state of Pennsylvania labored diligently to provide civilians and soldiers with ample supplies of clean, safe water. The wartime epidemics of waterborne diseases and dangerous shortages of fresh drinking sources would not be repeated at the Grand Reunion. Pictured here are water towers and a pump system within the Great Camp. (Courtesy George Grantham Bain Collection, Library of Congress)

of Gettysburg, Harrisburg, Sharpsburg, and others, should dire emergencies arise.[40]

This effort was not purely philanthropic. The War Department viewed the event as an opportunity to test procedures and equipage. For example, the larger and taller warm-weather hospital tents, observed the chief surgeon, were much cooler and more spacious than traditional all-weather enclosures, although they were "heavier, however, and not so acceptable when the transportation factor is concerned." The *Oswego Daily Palladium* offered a more jaundiced view, projecting, "the army of the future will find pleasure in the fact that while they may be shot to pieces, blown up by mines, and riddled by shells from enemies' fire, that the commissary department will be able to serve them promptly with the best that the Department affords." Yet the overriding reaction among the aging and infirm was a deep appreciation for the modern amenities and the government's attention to their personal needs. The thoroughness of preparation, commented one veteran, made the entire Reunion, "a sanitary object lesson." The *Pittsburgh Post-Gazette* went so far as to deem the place a "health resort" that added greatly to the pleasure of the aged participants and tourists alike.[41]

CHAPTER 4

The Need to Find

"I am so tired that I can't see, but I wouldn't have missed this trip for 20 years of my life."
—LETTER FROM VETERAN CLAUDE LELAND to his wife and family,
June 30, 1913, Claude G. Leland Collection (MS 2958.5741,
New York Historical Society)

Some simply could not wait to get started, so they created their own wake-up call. At 4:30 A.M., fifes, drums, and war whoops emanated from the Confederate side of the encampment. Those most adventurous decided to "invade" their Union counterparts. How this predawn lark did not result in a cranky melee of swinging canes is a mystery, but it did signal the strangely playful convention that prevailed when the men congregated in large numbers.[1]

By 5:30 A.M. the camp's electric lights had flickered off, and a warming sun ascended over Cemetery Ridge into a cloudless sky. Strong breezes swept through the tent city, pressing and billowing the canvas shelters, as if the encampment were taking its first deep breaths of morning air. Over at the depot, the day's first trains rolled in, bringing passengers from Washington State and Wisconsin. Camp bakers, cooks, and assistants finished prepping a colossal breakfast of bacon and eggs, boiled potatoes, fresh local fruit, fresh-baked bread, fried ham, and pistol-hot coffee. Over at the college, Pennsylvania's governor John Tener and staff were busy setting up offices. To monitor his prized event firsthand, Tener officially moved the state's seat of government to Gettysburg for the week.[2]

The sun, the breezes, and the smell of baking and cooking roused William Fickas and his Phoenix companions: Emil Ganz, Joshua Vinson, Wilber Phillips, Marion Abbott, Andrew Weaber, and J. J. Camp, out in the Arizona tents. With them as always was their chaperone William Hartranft. As they headed out to explore the battlefield, each expressed surprise at how, after initial moments of confusion, they could recognize places they had not seen in a half century. Such was a common discovery among veterans. "It is remarkable how long and well the soldiers remember every spot, every move, every order, every incident of a battle," remarked a reporter from North Carolina, "they would gather in groups and point to the scene."[3]

The Fickas octet strode through camp, past the teeming Meadeboro, and through the main square, coincidentally re-creating the famous irony of Gettysburg, where the North entered the battle from the south and the South came in from the north. Fickas was retracing the path of his artillery unit on day one, in which it rushed through the borough to establish a perimeter on the outskirts. His destination was Blocher's Knoll, a rise just beyond the northern edge of town. Upon this hill on July 1, Fickas's Battery G of the 4th US Artillery had tried to anchor a hastily formed line of infantry.[4]

This place was familiar to Emil Ganz and Joshua Vinson as well, for it was Ganz's 21st Georgia, Vinson's 35th Virginia Cavalry Battalion, and nearly the whole of Robert E. Lee's Second Corps that stormed this position from the north and bowled it over in short order.[5] Together Fickas, Vinson, and Ganz recounted what they saw and did. The conversation may have been most difficult for Fickas. It was his line that fractured that day. In fact it was Ganz's regiment, advancing from the northwest and heading for the rear of Blocher's Knoll that came closest to severing Battery G's line of escape. In the melee Fickas lost his commanding officer, Lt. Bayard Wilkeson, when a Confederate shell tore off one of the young officer's legs below the knee, a wound that would soon prove fatal. After the battle, Wilkeson's journalist father may have inspired one of the more powerful lines in Lincoln's immortal address. Hearing of his son's demise, the elder Wilkeson told his *New York Times* readers that the dead of Gettysburg may have given the nation "a second birth of freedom."[6]

Above: Panorama of the Great Camp looking eastward from Seminary Ridge. Faintly visible are the Round Tops (*right*) and train cars (*center left*)—part of the Gettysburg & Harrisburg Rail Line that ran diagonally through the encampment. (Panoramic Photograph Collection, Library of Congress)

At the time of the lieutenant's wounding, it was not yet evident that the nineteen-year-old would die, yet both Fickas and Vinson remembered that so many of the battery's horses had been killed that the crews had to drag the guns and caissons away by hand in a desperate attempt to escape. As Battery G had done that day, the small tour group went back through town and up Cemetery Hill. As they ascended, to their left they could see the famous arched gatehouse to Evergreen Cemetery, appearing much as it did on the evening of July 1. What looked far different was the ground beneath them: the long, thin semicircles of Union grave markers, emanating from the National Soldiers' Monument in front of them like ripples on a pond.[7]

Vinson admitted the scenery was beginning to affect him, mostly the marked difference between the beautified landscape and the macabre gravesites. "I could not believe that the north had lost so many men, until

Below: Gettysburg National Cemetery prepared for the Great Reunion, with US and state of Pennsylvania flags adorning the grave markers. The New York State Monument stands in the background. (*Fiftieth Anniversary of the Battle of Gettysburg: Report of the Pennsylvania Commission*)

I saw those monuments." Marion Abbott later offered a possible explanation for why Vinson felt so moved. The countryside, Abbott noticed, appeared much as it did when they arrived there in 1863. The Round Tops looked the same, as did Devil's Den, Meade's headquarters, the layout of the town. Even faces were recognizable. Abbott himself came across a fellow member of his regiment whom he had not seen since the war, "his beard now, snow white, was then jet black but it was of about the same length. . . . A red headed youth was unchanged as to his laughing eyes." The most noticeable change involved the headstones, being so abundant as to be inescapable and demoralizing in their multitudes. Altogether the cemetery contained 3,512 bodies, nearly a thousand of which were unknown.[8]

Compared to other national cemeteries (all of them depositories invented by the US Congress in 1862 to contain the war's mounting losses), Gettysburg's resting place was rather modest in size, especially compared to Arlington's 16,000, Nashville's 16,485, or Vicksburg's 17,000. Yet a sense of loss could be magnified incalculably if a survivor came across a familiar name. For Abbott, this would have been along Row 10, Section A, where his sergeant Philip Hamlin resided. Nearby were comrades Charles Baker, George Grands, Alonzo Hayden, plus twenty-nine others from his regiment whose bodies were identified, and twenty more who were not. Fickas may have also seen epitaphs he would have recognized, such as William Patton from the 4th US Artillery and William Tillotson from his hometown.[9]

How the veterans reacted to a familiar name varied widely, from quiet reflection to overt mourning. Discoveries were often difficult to process. One survivor was seen weeping next to a marker, saying to passersby, "he's under there." After several minutes of crying, the man slowly slumped over and lay upon the grass.[10]

Standing watch over the graves, the towering Soldiers' Monument offered a hawkish interpretation of human progress, personified by four youthful human statues at its base. One anthropomorphized War (as a pristine, idyllic figure), History (recording war), Peace (through war), and Prosperity (the sum of the preceding three). Atop the pillar above them stood the Genius of Peace, a Roman goddess armed with both laurel and sword. Often mistaken as the spot where Lincoln delivered the Gettysburg Address (the actual location being nearer the apex of Cemetery Hill in the civilian Evergreen Cemetery) the monument stood as a glorification of the deceased.[11]

Near this ornate tribute, Fickas likely turned around and surveyed the town, facing the same direction his battery had positioned itself against the Confederate pursuit at nightfall. As painful as his recollections may have been of that first twilight's defense, Fickas's memories of the following evening were likely far worse. It was then that Wilber Phillips could join the discussion. On the night of July 2, a hundred paces west and downhill from Battery G, Phillips and his 136th New York Regiment were positioned on the extreme left of the Union line along Taneytown Road. So tactically valued was Cemetery Hill that Fickas and his men were one of a dozen Union batteries ordered to defend the hill's crown, and Phillips was just one of thousands of infantrymen assigned to hold its base.[12]

Intent on crushing them with envelopment from the west, north, and east were eight regiments in gray, including H. H. Hodges's comrades in the 21st North Carolina. For a time, along East Cemetery Hill, the fighting turned hand to hand, indeed, primeval. Some men threw rocks, others used the butt of their rifles and clubbed their opponents to death. Mammalian instincts intertwined with modern technology to horrific effect. During the firefight, a private witnessed the impact of Union artillery upon a Confederate surge, with "heads, arms, and legs flying amid the dust and smoke. . . . It reminded me much of a wagon load of pumpkins drawn up a hill and the end gate coming out, and the pumpkins rolling and bounding down the hill." And still, for a time, remnants of the 21st North Carolina and others held the crest until darkness, when clouds of acrid smoke and utter confusion dissolved their assault. Such visions plagued Fickas and his companions as they stood in the morning sun upon a green and peaceful vista.[13]

Whether H. H. Hodges ever walked to where Fickas et al. were standing is unknown, but Cemetery Hill was not unknown to him. Several of his acquaintances, neighbors, and distant relatives were killed or wounded upon its slopes. As emotional as the retracing could be, those who returned to such places often cherished the multiple perspectives they shared with other survivors. Out of complicated memories, a collective sympathy could emerge, an awareness that each was not alone in his fear and confusion.[14]

The Fickas troupe moved on, threading its way through the chain of cars sputtering along the tarmac of Taneytown Road. Their next stop was easy to find. It consisted of a lone grove of trees surrounded by a stand of monuments. A crowd was already present, as there would be almost every hour of every day. This was the Bloody Angle. Fickas wanted to see where his fellow gunners from 4th US Artillery stood as they faced the onslaught of Pickett's Charge. While his Battery G fired from Cemetery Hill, Lt. Alonzo Cushing's Battery A delivered from point-blank range just behind the low stone wall. Coming to this place for the first time in fifty years, Fickas did something remarkable—he simply listened.[15]

Present were numerous survivors of Pickett's division, recalling how the "withering, enfilading fire" tore through them as they marched forward. Fickas knew that part of that barrage emanated from his guns. As he listened to the men he once tried to kill, or more accurately, a different William Fickas tried to kill, he looked upon a position that had remained implanted in his mind. His memory fixated not upon the famed Copse of Trees, nor the Angle, nor Seminary Ridge; it focused upon an innocuous fence row along Emmitsburg Road. He vividly remembered how nearly every Confederate who crossed that line on July 3 became a casualty, partly from his work. This was Battery G's primary target during the assault. During the engagement, the fence created a clogging effect, bunching men into a nearly straight, compacted line stretching down and away from his position. Whether landing short or long, Fickas's shells could hardly miss. A Confederate described the experience: "shells amongst us, shells over us and shells around us tore our bleeding ranks with ghastly gaps. . . . The ground roared and rumbled like a great storm."[16]

Whether the thought of "national reconciliation" crossed his mind at this point, Fickas did not say, but he did express empathy for individuals he once tried to harm, and who tried to harm him. What may have helped Fickas process his visions of destruction were the very men he was encountering. Each served as tangible proof that many of his targets had survived and indeed lived long lives.[17] If there was one thing that Fickas personally sought but did not find at Cemetery Hill and Cemetery Ridge, it was a fellow survivor of the 4th US Artillery, but there was still time for that. Leaving the Angle, Fickas and his team headed southward, past the Codori farm and the Great Tent far off to their right, and just beyond the domed behemoth of the Pennsylvania Monument to their left, the landscape triggering memories at nearly every step.

So went the day, with hundreds of small groups like Fickas's wandering near and far. From its inception, the Grand Reunion was not some unified celebration; it was more a litany of small search parties. One who immediately saw this was New York journalist Lindsay Denison, noticing time and again how "two, three, four, a half dozen would wander up and down the lines trying to find in farmhouse gardens, made-over fields, new grown woods, the exact spots where they escaped death." The 20th Maine's exploits on Little Round Top were not yet famous, but the fight's gruesome specifics were indelible to those involved. Claude Leland helped a veteran of the 20th Maine find the regiment's monument, a tree-veiled and modest cenotaph resting on the far side of the rise. "When I took him over the brow of the hill," said Leland, "and he caught sight of the stone embankments he helped build and the granite shaft just where the colors stood, it was too much for him. He broke down and cried like a child."[18]

Throughout the day, train whistles announced the arrival of yet more people pouring into the packed townscape. From predawn to near midnight, a Western Maryland trainload came in no fewer than twenty times, and the Reading Line made more than thirty passenger deliveries, dropping off nearly twenty-two thousand people altogether on this day. Adding to the masses, many nearby veterans arrived by car. Swarms of small parties packed in roadsters and coupes drove in to see the crowds, or as one group said, "just for the trip." An estimated fifteen thousand veterans from Pennsylvania alone were already in camp, with more on the way.[19]

To reduce the chances of being overrun with unmanageable numbers, the War Department and Anniversary Commission opted to limit access to the camp proper. Official regulations stated in no uncertain terms, "no woman, nor child, nor any man not such veteran, will be given such food, shelter or entertainment therein." The strategy also stemmed from the desire to create a military-style atmosphere. There were army cots and blankets in army tents, guarded by US regular infantry and cavalry equipped with rifles and pistols. All scheduled speakers were politicians and high-ranking officers.[20]

Noticeably, the veterans advanced a more civilian milieu. Most Federal veterans, including Allen and Fickas, wore civilian clothes throughout the week. Despite orders to the contrary, many men North and South brought family members along. Female relatives of Union and Confederate officers stayed at the Lutheran Seminary. Of the forty-five attendees from the 3rd Pennsylvania Cavalry, around thirty came with their wives and children and sat together with them during the regiment's reunion in the Great Tent on July 1. Union veteran George Duke noted that "the rebs brought a lot of women with them." The sizable presence of females made more than a few of the men sentimental, and not for warfare. Said one Mr. Townshend of Texas, "I fell in love with the good women who were at the reunion." A. F. McCord of Pickens, South Carolina, admitted, "a number of ladies called to see us in our tents and invited us to see their palatial homes, which was enjoyed by those who accepted the invitation." A veteran from Pittsburgh happily informed his wife, "I can take you along this time, Jennie."[21]

After seeing the numbers of women present, several men lamented they had not brought their loved ones. Hodges was rarely without his Martha. Waldron had been with Fannie since 1865. "I wish Jane was here," said a man walking near the Copse of Trees. "She had a harder time than I did enduring the war." Many dealt with the absence by creating proxy kinships. Heman Allen's cohorts from the 13th Vermont acknowledged: "before leaving home, it was understood that none but veterans would be allowed in camp, but when we got there and were located, we found these restrictions were not fully carried out, as many citizens and even ladies were admitted. Frequently we had lady callers. One day a prominent lady and her two daughters called on us and we invited them to dinner. This invitation was accepted. We arranged a table and seats under the fly tent situated at the head of the street."[22]

Seeing Gettysburg impacted these civilians as well, as it often provided solace similar to what the veterans were experiencing. Joseph Seaton's daughter Lena traveled with him all the way from Kansas, as did the wife and daughter of J. S. Lewis from Georgia and William Larrabee's son from Iowa, as well as relatives of George Gordon Meade.[23] Their journey brought them to a place that shaped much of their own lives. Literature scholar Marianne Hirsch would later describe such groups as a "generation of postmemory," or those affected by a traumatic event they did not directly experience. Also known as secondary post-traumatic stress disorder, the phenomenon produces feelings of alienation, confusion, fear, frustration, and guilt. After the Civil War, veteran care fell principally upon families, and entire households lived with the physical and mental torment that beset relatives who fought in the war. Rare was the community that did not contain living reminders such as amputees, sufferers of "Old Soldiers Heart" (acute combat syndrome and post-traumatic stress disorder), those who self-medicated through alcohol and opiates, the withdrawn, and the occasionally violent. Lingering, too, was bereavement for the seven hundred thousand who never returned.[24] Millions of noncombatants sought closure no less than veterans did. Said one woman walking along Emmitsburg Road, "I wasn't expected, but I just couldn't help coming. Jim was killed along here somewhere, I think it must have been about here. He did not come back to me, but I am going to him."[25] Many scoured the National Cemetery for lost loved ones, including a woman hoping to find the name of her husband. Her odds were long, because he had been classified as missing in action ever since the battle.[26]

Magdalena Luhm of Wisconsin came with her family to revisit their old farm between Gettysburg and Chambersburg. She was just six in 1863 when she looked out on a summer night and saw flashes of artillery enveloping Culp's Hill. Luhm recalled how her home "was soon crowded

A large contingent of women stands with veterans along the encampment's 36th Street West, in the North Carolina section near Confederate Avenue. Contrary to official rules, women toured the Great Camp nearly at will, and veterans widely insisted that they be welcomed participants in the Jubilee. (Courtesy National Photo Company Collection, Library of Congress)

with soldiers who were wounded, sick, or hungry to the starving point, and it was many days before that neighborhood was free from the stains of the terrible battle." She found her return rejuvenating, however, because she was able to revisit many of her childhood friends, and she could see firsthand how her native landscape had healed, as "grass has covered most of the scars, and the once bloody field is not unlike a vast and beautiful park." Survivors like Luhm sought a new Gettysburg, one that affirmed that life was more resilient than death.[27]

Georgia Wade McClellan, Jennie Wade's sister, traveled with her son and husband from Denison, Iowa, to retrace her days and nights of the battle. She reentered the room where her sister had died, where her infant son (mere weeks old) lay as bullets pierced the walls. She recalled how the house and the entire town became a hospital for the living, and she walked to Devil's Den, where she helped drag three wounded soldiers from its crevasses. "I was not twenty-two years old," she said, "I nursed the wounded for the remainder of the war." When news spread that Jennie Wade's sister was present, scores of journalists, sightseers, and veterans swarmed upon her, asking her to recount her and her sister's trials, over and over. To the point of exhaustion, Georgia tried to accommodate as many veterans as she could.[28]

Nannie Randolph Heth, daughter of the late brigadier general Henry Heth, made her way to the southwest corner of the encampment in search of his old command, which included Mississippians, Tennesseans, Virginians, and others. One of his brigades consisted entirely of North Carolinians, and when she reached the headquarters of their section, her presence initially prompted great excitement and a growing crowd of grateful admirers of her late father. In a short while, the men began to weep in memory of all whom they had lost, including her father in 1899, and Nannie wept with them.[29]

Undeniably, many veterans were female, and not just the few score who posed as men in the ranks. Thousands worked as civilian commissary agents, emergency relief personnel, and trauma nurses. The Reunion itself revealed an expanding presence of women in the medical field and their critical role in public healthcare, albeit in an increasingly cemented division of gender roles. During the war, the majority of nurses were male. In the aid stations and field hospitals located across the battlefield park, most health workers were female: seventy-one of them, all of whom were professionally trained members of the American Red Cross. Neither that institution nor any nursing college existed in the United States in the 1860s. By the time of the Reunion, there were scores of such organizations, including the Bellevue Hospital School of Nursing (founded 1873), the Johns Hopkins School of Nursing (1883), the Army Nurse Corps (1901), and the Minnesota University Nursing Program (1909). For men of age and subjected to taxing camp and climactic conditions, services of the nursing corps at the Reunion were rightly praised as lifesaving. Veteran John Delaney was not hyperbolic in declaring that among all the provisions made at the anniversary, the aid stations "won most enthusiastic praise from all."[30]

Regardless, marginalization of females persisted. None of the ten doctors present were women. Organizers also brought in twenty-five coal miners from the anthracite regions of Pennsylvania to help carry stretchers and supplies, assist heatstroke victims, and conduct other work that allegedly, as one reporter worded it, "the women nurses could not hope to do." When asked what the world would look like in one hundred years, playwright Mrs. Barney Hemmick of Washington, DC, predicted that by 2013 on the 150th anniversary of the battle, it would be likely that "both men and women would publicly wear trousers," but a Victorian feminine ideal held firmly for the time being.[31]

Not all shared the assumption of the gender's frailty, including many Gettysburg residents. One of the more tragic but lesser-known outcomes of the battle, as historian Gregory Coco noted, involved the dearth of medical support after the fight was over. Anticipating that the decisive engagement was still to come, both the Army of Northern Virginia and the Army of the Potomac took somewhere between 70 and 90 percent of their ambulances, doctors, and medical supplies with them as they maneuvered southward, leaving behind some two thousand townspeople to care for twenty-seven thousand wounded. The dead alone outnumbered civilians by more than three to one. Residents and wounded recalled how the town had involuntarily become "one vast hospital," with hundreds of homes and buildings occupied by the dead and dying.[32]

In recognition of their work in saving many of the critically injured, seven women formed the nucleus of their own civilian nurses' reunion within the Reunion, a group that swelled to at least thirty. They headquartered at the home of Mrs. Salome M. Stewart, a Gettysburg native whose house had become an aid station after the battle. Fellow nightingales came from as far away as Philadelphia, and veterans traveled from a thousand miles and more in search of them. John Clevenger, sergeant of Company L, 1st New Jersey Cavalry, wanted to find a woman he encountered on July 3 near Gen. John Sedgewick's headquarters. He vividly recalled her being covered in soot from powder smoke and wearing a dress torn by bullets. Taking her to a makeshift hospital, he found that she was stunned but unhurt, and she immediately began to care for the wounded there. Unfortunately, Clevenger never learned her name or her fate. W. F. Hubbard trekked all the way from Los Angeles in search of a local who had quite possibly saved his life when he became one of the engagement's severely wounded. He survived, by his own assessment, because a female resident came to his aid and cared for him through the first critical hours. In the chaos of the battle he soon lost contact with her and never learned who she was. Fifty years later, despite searching for several days, he was unable to find her again.[33]

What could also not be found, among the growing host of granite memorials and bronze adornments, was a single marker that recognized the roles of women. Vexed by the oversight, Pennsylvania veterans called for a national monument at Gettysburg. The idea quickly gained support across the camp and reached the pages of several national newspapers. One journalist fumed at the omission, warning readers, "the hardship, the suffering, the agony of the women who waited in the war homes of the nation may never be told," but also offered hope that "some day a grateful Government will erect a monument that will pierce the blue heavens from Gettysburg's stateliest, sunniest slope."[34] The adamant writer happened to be Helen Longstreet, widow of Lee's 1st Corps commander. Much celebrated for her appearance at the anniversary, Longstreet parlayed her notoriety, and her work as a columnist, to attain virtually unlimited access to the encampment. While most newsprint covering her presence emphasized her apparent kindness and public support of the controversial Daniel Sickles, her own writing overtly questioned why the Anniversary Commission and US Congress did not make the event into a recognition and reunion of veterans' families, let alone provide any accommodations for spouses of the common soldier. She noted, "today, just one-half of America's Civil War soldiers are here; the stronger half are waiting back home to be told of the happenings of this day.... It was the women who suffered most during the war, and I am sorry they are not here."[35]

There were of course many female figures present on the monuments, often posed at the zenith of such shrines, but these were invariably idealized, alluring, youthful figures advancing the metaphor of a nation needing to be rescued. The most prominent ornaments were the feminine Genius of Peace atop the National Cemetery Soldiers' Monument and the Goddess of Victory and Peace standing on the domed Pennsylvania Memorial.

While female contributions were ubiquitous topics of conversation among veterans, official reports (including the authoritative volume from the Pennsylvania Commission) minimized women's involvement at the Reunion and in the war itself.[36] Compare this to the actions of veterans of John Buford's cavalry division. On returning to Gettysburg, F. A. Easton of the 6th New York Cavalry sought local women in their fifties and early sixties, in hopes of finding the ones "who, as school children, scattered flowers in the paths of Buford's cavalry and sang patriotic songs as they entered the town June 30, 1863." Easton was led to believe that perhaps a dozen or more were still alive, and if he could arrange it, he was going to ask them to sing the same songs again to his fellow survivors. Said one cavalryman, "I can remember that when we first went into town in squads scouting to see if any of the enemy were there, we were met by a lot of children, little bits of things from seven to ten years old, waving paper flags and singing 'John Brown's Body.'" Fellow troopers canvassed the town in search of those once "little bits of things" who might still be alive. "I think it would be nice," said a Major Wheeler, "to have a talk with them."[37]

Their search produced six residents who were part of that original welcoming committee—Mrs. Salome Stewart, Miss Sally Hearns, Mrs. Rupp, Miss Carrie Young, Mrs. Shields, and Mrs. William Tawney. Their discovery soon led to a reunification in the Great Tent, consisting of Buford's riders, the six women, a collection of musicians, and onlookers intrigued by the lively, spontaneous gathering. Once inside, the small crowd invited the women to stand atop the large stage. "I'm afraid we can't sing like we sang 50 years ago," said one. The veterans responded, "We don't care; just sing again."[38]

The musicians began to play "Rally Round the Flag, Boys," and the women slowly joined, their voices barely audible amidst the din of the instruments. After a few measures, the assembly implored the band to stop, and the lyrics from the modest sextet began to float into the mass. The crowd fell silent. Some of the men began sobbing.[39] One by one the soldiers approached the stage and queried for more information about what the women remembered. One individual sought Carrie Young in particular and asked, "Ain't you the young lady that was on that dry goods box singing that song when our troop came into the square? I think you was." Despite his desire for Young to be his specific connection to that time and place, she shook her head and confessed that she could not recall.[40]

Another from the 8th Illinois Cavalry came up and told the women that he had a memento from that first encounter, a purple ribbon that he had kept ever since: "I kinder just wondered if the little bit of a gal that gave me the purple ribbon I have got in my box back home was here. She ran out in front of my horse with some flowers. I got down off the horse and she gave me that purple ribbon out of her hair and asked me to wear it in the fight, I laughed and told her there wasn't going to be a fight, but she told me there was. She was right. I wanted to tell her so."[41]

When none of the women came forth, the hopeful man returned to his seat, visibly dejected. Such was the prevailing behavior. Men who soon would be showered with speeches about masculinity and sacrifice spent most of their time seeking out the intimate and tangible. Foremost, they sought living reminders of their experience, any confirmation of their personal survival and the survival of others they once knew.[42]

Yet the official schedule made no place for the "fairer sex," viewing them as essentially unrelated to the proceedings, if not potentially disruptive, especially when it came to acknowledging the role of women in the public sphere. When praising the support of Boy Scouts at the event, the Associated Press added, "the lads have had experience in handling crowds, having done some notable service in suppressing disorder during the suffrage parade [in Washington, DC,] March 2 last." This gender preference did not prevent women from actively participating, including suffrage workers. Taking advantage of the large crowds and ensuing newspaper coverage, a group of women's rights advocates "invaded" the celebration, as one reporter wrote, "to spread the votes-for-women propaganda among the veterans."[43] Support for the movement had been growing steadily since the war, especially among western territories and states. Wyoming approved female suffrage in 1869, and endorsements from other regions slowly followed: Colorado in 1893; Idaho and Utah by 1896; Washington in 1910; with California, Kansas, Oregon, and Fickas's adopted Arizona adding to the eastward tide. On the same day that the South Dakota Senate appropriated $10,000 to help finance the Gettysburg Jubilee, it also overwhelmingly approved a statewide referendum on granting women the vote. Days before the Reunion, Gov. Edward Dunne of Illinois signed his state's recently passed suffrage measure into law, a bill supported by the assembly's many members of the Progressive Party as well as its three representatives of the Socialists. The signing made the Land of Lincoln the first state east of the Mississippi to grant the right for women to vote in presidential elections.[44]

Stalwart holdouts were states of the Deep South and the Eastern Seaboard, but a large proportion of the veterans supported the measure. Near the Great Tent, suffrage organizers erected a modest information station, complete with petitions, pamphlets, buttons, and banners. By the end of the week, the reformers collected twelve thousand signatures from thirty-two states in support of an amendment. One old soldier said he was motivated to sign because of what he had seen during his years in uniform. "Any woman that was a nurse in the civil war," he declared, "ought to vote."[45]

As evening approached, a reporter from the *Gettysburg Times* reckoned there were at least forty thousand soldiers already present, with trains, cars, and carriages bringing more by the minute. Most were establishing a pattern that would continue through the week, showing an inclination to explore on their own. If there was a major problem to be found, it involved losing one's bearings. A late arrival found his way into the encampment and could not figure his way out. "Where's them monuments I've been seeing on paper? I be blamed if I don't believe it's a durned trick. There ain't any monuments here. There's nothing here but blamed tents."[46] The camp was so enormous, and homogeneous, that the precise grid of streets did not prevent individuals from getting lost. Journalist Lindsay Denison believed the issue caused at least five thousand individuals to spend their first night sleeping under the stars and without as much as a blanket.[47] One such wanderer belonged to Waldron's 28th Virginia, who stumbled upon survivors of the 1st Minnesota. The men welcomed him in, and after stories of their encounters, the Virginian learned that his regimental battle flag was in St. Paul, a prize of war. The man fell asleep upon a cot in the Minnesota tents and stayed the night. Upon waking, he sat on the side of a bed and roused the occupant, and he confessed, "Since some of you Yanks had to get that flag I'm glad it was you all. You are pretty good people."[48]

CHAPTER 5

"Veterans' Day"

⎯⎯⎯⎯ ☀ ⎯⎯⎯⎯

"It is not merely that human slavery was destroyed. It is not merely that the doctrine of secession was crushed. It was not merely that the North bayoneted the South back into the Union and established the supremacy of the national authority. . . . The baptism of blood was indeed a consecration."
—*WASHINGTON POST*, July 1, 1913

The official start of the anniversary brought a rise in temperature, humidity, and the number of tourists. In Vermont's section of camp, Heman Allen spent much of his time in Tent Number 4, the ad hoc headquarters of his regiment. In between conversations with neighbors and visitors, Allen and his associates tended to a tiny family nearby. A nest of birds had made their home in the mouth of an artillery piece along Confederate Avenue. On occasion, a chick would stumble out and fall, prompting Allen and company to return it to its siblings. A third of a mile south, H. H. Hodges and his neighbor Moses Waldron, a few streets beyond, partook of yet another lavish breakfast. On the east side of the tent city, William Fickas ventured out in search of old comrades.[1]

A popular spot for many of them on July 1 was Seminary Ridge along West Confederate Avenue, "Pickett's Charge" point of departure on July 3. Its attraction today, and every day, was its long canopy of mature shade trees that helped deflect the punishing sun. Nearly every morning, the corridor developed its own festive atmosphere. Refreshment peddlers and paperboys offered their wares. Itinerate preachers evangelized to the passersby. On this day, well before noon, the mass of veterans and tourists was so thick along the shaded boulevard that automobiles were unable to pass through.[2]

Formal activities, consisting of brass band music and speeches in the Great Tent, were to begin in the early afternoon, the hottest part of the day. Set to give the welcoming address was US secretary of war Lindley Garrison, an accomplished legal mind who favored an aggressive overseas military policy. The secretary could be viewed as a reasonable choice to inaugurate the proceedings, since the preserved battlefield was under the jurisdiction of the War Department and nearly all encampment food and shelter came compliments of Uncle Sam. Garrison himself might not have been an ideal lead for Veterans Day, considering that he had never served in the military, yet his credentials became somewhat of a moot point. As it turned out, the official program was not what interested the old soldiers most. Setting the pattern for the next four days, aside from being attentive to the dinner bell, most veterans made their own schedule. Queried by a hometown paper, one of Hodges's fellow North Carolinians said, "How did we put in our time? We scattered."[3]

Most political figures and papers with nationalist leanings were partially correct in painting the Reunion as a quest for reconciliation, but the goal among veterans did not involve being actors in a grand gesture of forgiveness between North and South. What most sought were reconciliations between their own past and present. "The arrival of the Secretary of War and dozens of other prominent guests stirred but passing interest in the hearts of the men of Meade and Lee," noticed a Philadelphia journalist. "The vast majority, and by the vast majority let it be known as 99 out of every 100 veterans, spent the day out on the familiar old battlefield, in the tents of their comrades, or looking for the spots they occupied fifty years ago."[4] The ratio was an exaggeration, but not by much. An Indiana reporter estimated that less than a quarter of those in the tent were vets. Missouri transplant J. B. Furman spoke for many when he admitted, "somehow I couldn't listen to set speeches. I concluded I could read the speeches in the newspapers. I wanted to wander over the grounds of the battlefield with my comrades, and see the wonderful transformation which fifty years had wrought."[5]

Furman's witnessing a "wonderful transformation" meant a great deal to him and others. The word "battlefield" of course contradicts reality. The war's ten thousand engagements, large and small, transpired in towns; on people's farms and in their homes; alongside churches, warehouses, business districts, and roads; and upon the high seas and rivers. Citizen-soldiers themselves wrote about severe destruction. For most, their last recollections of Gettysburg was of a horrific dystopia. Upon their return, they found a serene setting, a vibrant town, and its growing battlefield "park," very much alive with people of all ages, a vista adorned with growing orchards and quilted with pristine fields. This transformation made it possible for Allen, Fickas, Hodges, Waldron, and others to simultaneously mourn and find peace. Poignantly, the Indiana Reunion Commission's official report emphasized how the new "battlefield" had been "laid out and beautified in all the ways known to the most expert landscape artists."[6]

For many, the return to Gettysburg helped them address a lingering guilt of survivorship. On this first official day of the anniversary, Helen Longstreet came upon a Pennsylvania man standing beside a cherry tree near Cemetery Ridge, who was undergoing this process of purging horrific memories and reinserting humane ones. "It was right here," he told her, "there was a brave fellow from Michigan I was mighty fond of. We were resting after the repulse of Pickett's Charge and wondering whether we would have to follow those Johnnie Rebs back into Virginia." He then relayed how the men were eating cherries when "a stray shell directed by the devil snuffed out the life of the Michigan boy soldier. I took from his pocket the picture of the little girl who was waiting in her faraway Michigan home and sent it back to her, with a lock of her dead soldier's hair."[7] Psychiatrist Robert Jay Lifton finds that in cases in which people survive deadly experiences yet lose someone they know in the process, a critical means of coping is to understand that "survival is an achievement." Lifton notes that survivorship in itself is not necessarily an emancipation from past horrors; the persons involved have agency to seek their personal level of functionality, ranging from denial and numbing to introspection.[8] The supportive environment of the Reunion empowered individuals to move further along the growth side of the spectrum.

The pilgrimage could also represent a desire to forgive oneself for past actions. Marcus Trotter ventured from Parsons, Kansas, with strong memories of his time in the 3rd Indiana Cavalry. He wanted to identify the exact location where he stood on the battle's first day, where he felt utterly helpless. "One of the most pathetic things I saw was the killing of three brothers by the name of Lewis," he remembered. By Trotter's assessment, the first of them fell from the work of a sharpshooter. When the victim's brother tried to crawl out and rescue him, another rifle shot terminated the effort. "When the third brother attempted to reach their bodies," Trotter recalled, "an Indiana mother was childless." But the most punishing memory for Trotter was what followed. "We left their bodies there." The extent to which his departure affected Trotter thereafter is ultimately unknowable. What can be measured are the distance (twelve hundred miles) and time (fifty years) he traversed to return to that specific site and memory. For him, the act of remembering the brothers, and revisiting the place of their shared demise, can at least be considered a personal attempt at catharsis.[9]

In a similar incident, Samuel Marks returned to the place at which he left a sibling behind. As a teenager, Samuel accompanied his brother Thomas in joining the 53rd North Carolina Infantry. At Gettysburg, their regiment was charging a Federal position when Samuel saw his brother die. "I hadn't time to stop when Tom was shot," confessed Samuel. He felt some consolation in making this journey back, the first time he saw Gettysburg since that day. Daniel Krebs came all the way from Watts, California, to see where he fell wounded and where his brother had perished. Dr. J. A. Marshall of Alexandria, Virginia, came searching for information concerning the disappearance of his brother Col. James K. Marshall, who vanished during Pickett's Charge. The doctor himself marched into the melee as part of a nearby battalion. At the Reunion, Daniel desperately sought out members of Pettigrew's Brigade in hopes that someone could tell him of his brother's fate.[10]

Although the veteran could decipher this dual reality of past and present, much could be lost in translation for those who were not subjected to the trauma firsthand. As veteran Theodore Rose feared, "The visitor to the battlefield of Gettysburg, 50 years after, gets but a faint idea of the devastation and horrors of war. . . . The kindly healing of nature, aided by the Battlefield Memorial Association, has converted what was once a place of strife and horror into a landscape of quiet beauty and repose. . . . In short, it is a great battlefield turned into a beautiful cemetery and park . . . but no extensive ruins remain."[11] Consequently, for the uninitiated, the decorated vista could be interpreted however the mind desired. For militarists, it could read as glorification and validation, fiction as fact. The attraction for tourists included the draw of inherent drama, hero worship and idolatry, or simply a sterilized version of "history" that did not offend the senses.

Precisely how many non-veterans were present on the first day remains unknown, but the Reunion's attraction was considerable. Perhaps to entice a greater turnout, the *Gettysburg Times* claimed that not more than four thousand had made it thus far and that "eighty percent of the homes in town have been prepared to take lodgers." In stark contrast, the *Gettysburg Compiler* contended, "the main streets were as thickly crowded as Broadway, New York or Market Street, Philadelphia." The *Washington Times* insisted the total number of tourists was closer to two hundred thousand. The *Fort Wayne Daily News* painted a similar image of inundation, warning, "there is not enough for the visitors to eat and no place for them to sleep. Corridors, porches, and even large closets of the hotels and hundreds of private homes are filled up."[12]

Somewhere in between resided the truth, and even then the number oscillated. Some tourists visited but a few hours, while others stayed for the duration. From locals to world travelers, the anniversary was a once-in-a-lifetime sight to behold, a national and unprecedented event hyped for months and laden with enough famous figures to render even the most stoic citizen curious. But for the veteran, there was a danger of overselling Gettysburg, for it could easily devolve from a place of healing to a weekender's campground. Joseph Stone of Vermont found the inundation remarkable yet somewhat unsettling. In a letter to his wife, Stone reflected, "there was lots of people that came to visit the camp last night, old and young all want to shake hands. Bands playing, autos going on all streets and you can hardly hear yourself speak."[13] George Duke of the 104th Pennsylvania marveled at the crowds but felt as if he were at their mercy: "We had to move as the crowd carried us, and it was 50,000 and then some."[14]

John Catlin of Oregon expressed greater concern over the potential long-term effect: "The battlefield has been kept in a remarkable state of preservation, although some places have been fixed up beyond recollection. It is fast becoming a great resort for tourists."[15]

The park could, and did, serve as a platform for promoting and romanticizing warfare. Arriving this day was the 3rd US Artillery, which brought its guns for official salutes. When they weren't firing into the sky, the outfit carted about the camp with horse-drawn caissons. Meant to impress, the mock blasts may have stunned the veterans, who could clearly recall the effects of very real shells upon humans and horses.[16] In their early teens, Allen, Fickas, Hodges, and Waldron could have safely assumed they would be civilians for the entirety of their lives. The official approach at the Reunion was to refer to the veterans as a mighty, immortal singularity, a symbiotic universal soldier. The truth was that 97 percent of Civil War combatants were civilians before, after, and in many ways during the war itself. Since childhood, Hodges worked on a farm, an occupation he still practiced at age seventy. Waldron also farmed in his younger days. Fickas had become a skilled cooper before the war. Allen earned wages in a dry goods store.[17]

In the ongoing search for familiar faces among the crowds, men strode about with various medallions, patches, and ribbons pinned to their tunics. Instructions sent to them encouraged all participants "to wear their Army, Corps, Division, Brigade, and Society Badges, as a means of identification." In practice, the veterans chose to show even greater initiative. One North Carolina man, bedecked in a Confederate hat and gray suit, wore a large sash with his regiment's name and number upon it, like a walking billboard in search of old clients. He would have been hard to miss regardless, standing a lanky 6'4" among men whose average height was around 5'6". In tribute to his father who served as a Union division commander at Gettysburg, Gen. Alexander Hays's son set up headquarters at 330 Baltimore Street. To mark the location, the son flew the very flag that his father's command used during its stand against Pickett's Charge, so that the general's men could congregate and find each other.[18] More commonly, veterans simply called out as they walked about the camp, shouting names of their own hometowns, companies, or regiments, patiently hoping for responses in the affirmative. Another strategy was to survey the tents, a process made somewhat complicated by the Reunion Commission's and the War Department's insistence that the men quarter with the state in which they presently lived rather than the state from which they hailed in wartime.[19] Notably, many gravitated away from their assigned spots and went searching for their old home states. Sometimes it worked. Scouting through the Maryland camp along Seminary Ridge, Edwin Selvage came upon an individual he thought he recognized. "Don't you know me?" Selvage asked the man, a Mr. W. G.

Delashmutt. "Wait a minute," Deslashmutt responded, "You were in the First Maryland Cavalry." Both men did belong to the same regiment and company. They soon realized that they had not seen each other since the Battle of Pollard's Farm, Virginia, in the spring of 1864. Instantly they recalled the very moment they were separated. Selvage explicitly remembered seeing his friend being shot in the chest and hearing Delashmutt call out to him, "They are pumping bullets at us." Upon reuniting, the two embraced.[20]

Camped far away from his old units, William Fickas struggled to make his own reconnections. A search for his fellow gunners from the US 4th Artillery in the US Regular Army section turned up no one, so he asked for directions to Indiana's allotted spot. Guides pointed him to the southeast corner toward the Great Tent. Working his way through the avenues and across the tracks of the Western Maryland Railroad, he eventually reached 35th Street, a six-hundred-foot-long gravel road and its seventy-four shelters pitched for the Hoosiers. From tent to tent, Fickas called, "Is there anybody here from the Fourteenth Indiana?" He eventually found a man sitting at the back of an enclosure, his snow-white beard hanging from a sun-reddened and weary face. "I'm here, Frank, the only one," said the respondent, calling Fickas by his middle name. "Come in." The voice was that of Charlie Meyerhoff, Fickas's former first lieutenant. The reuniting would be one of their fondest moments of the week. There would be others. Altogether there were twenty-one survivors of the 14th Indiana bivouacked along the lane, many of whom fought alongside Fickas's battery on Cemetery Hill. After years in relative solitude, he was soon surrounded by those who intrinsically understood what he had endured.[21]

Fickas's fellow Arizonan Joshua Vinson was not as fortunate. The long journey from Phoenix and lengthy battlefield excursion the day before greatly weakened him. Rendered sick and bedridden, he spent the remainder of the Reunion prostrate in his tent, as Fickas and the others from Phoenix cared for him in shifts. Vinson became distraught, not so much for being sick but because he had not yet seen anyone from his old 35th Virginia Cavalry Battalion and could not search for them. He sent the word out to their tents on the other side of the encampment, but none came to see him. At the end of the Reunion, having failed to reunite with anyone from his old unit, a resigned Vinson hypothesized that the few survivors from his regiment either forgot who he was or never really knew him.[22]

Predominant was this desire to remember and to be remembered. One Wisconsin man came looking for any living member of eighteen Confederate prisoners he had guarded after the battle. After several days in camp, he was still searching. The longing to see at least one of them alive may have stemmed from an awareness of how deadly prison camps often were, especially by the latter half of the war. The breakdown of the prisoner exchange by 1863, largely caused by marked disagreements on how African American POWs should be treated, rapidly swelled prison camp populations far beyond capacity. As a result, on average, a man who entered the Battle of Gettysburg stood a one-in-twenty-three chance of being killed in action, while a person entering a POW camp during the war saw his chances of dying slip to one in seven.[23]

Robert Drummond of the 111th New York credited much of his survival to the treatment he received from the men who captured him. Apprehended by North Carolinians on Gettysburg's first day, Drummond came to the Reunion with the singular desire to express his gratitude for their kindness. His mission brought him to the North Carolina headquarters and Col. Archibald Boyden, with whom Drummond corresponded several times as the anniversary neared. Entering the modest fly tent and finding Boyden therein, an enthusiastic Drummond began to recite the names of those he remembered, especially that of Green Eller, who exceeded even the most generous of captors. Boyden, too, recalled the name, as he came from the same county as Eller and remembered him as a "fine soldier." After sharing memories of Eller's many attributes, Drummond asked if he had made it the Reunion, to which Boyden essentially said "almost." Eller had died the year before. Hearing the news, Drummond broke down and "wept like a child," recalling how Eller treated his Union captives "with every consideration and kindness possible for one man to give another."[24]

Former POWs at the Reunion likely numbered in the thousands. For these survivors, their mutual sense of empathy was palpable, especially on July 1, during the official gathering of the United Prisoners of War.[25] Possibly in attendance, Fickas's companion Emil Ganz had been captured near Sharpsburg, Maryland. He was eventually incarcerated in Elmira (a.k.a., "Hellmira") in New York, in conditions so foul that inmates resorted to using rats as currency, and disease often claimed ten men a day. Unable to endure the privations, Ganz took the oath of loyalty to the Union in January 1865 and was released. J. F. Lightburn, formerly of the 31st Virginia, was a survivor of Camp Chase in Ohio, where small-pox, dysentery, and exposure killed more than twenty-two hundred. In many ways, Lightburn never fully recovered from his time. He still carried a Union bullet in his arm, and he said of himself, "I am still a Rebel prisoner."[26] Revisiting Gettysburg weighed heavily upon James H. Armstrong of Ottawa, Kansas, partly because of his time in captivity. He and several of his comrades from the 75th Ohio had been captured at Gettysburg sometime around 7 P.M. on the second day. Armstrong was nineteen at the time. He and eight others from his company were eventually taken to Andersonville. After a year, seven of them were dead.[27]

Despite their hardships, many former captives were able and willing to talk about their experiences, because so many around them underwent similar trials. Among them were Moses Waldron and William Gooley. Waldron was briefly held in Richmond's Libby Prison at the end of the war when that infamous Confederate site became property of the US Army. Gooley, taken at Saylor's Creek during the run to Appomattox, was first sent to Point Lookout, Maryland, then the Old Capitol Prison in Washington, and finally to Johnson's Island, Ohio.[28]

Politicos and press overlooked this and many other "minor" reunions in favor of the pomp and pageantry of the Great Tent kickoff event at 2 P.M. A capacity crowd of nearly thirteen thousand (perhaps half of whom were veterans) filled the floor and bleachers, and the stage creaked from nearly two hundred dignitaries seated upon the elevated platform. At the very center of the tent, a brass band played martial music, while the packed gathering tried to fan away the heat.[29]

At the top of the hour, Col. James Martinus Schoonmaker walked to the rostrum and attempted to quiet the crowd. As chairman of the Pennsylvania State Commission, he gazed out upon a moment that was as much his creation as anyone else's. Barrel chested, with a calm demeanor and billowing mustache, he exuded paternal confidence. In practice, he was the very manifestation of power. A millionaire magnate in the coke and coal industry, and vice president of the Pittsburgh and Lake Erie Railroad, he rose to the board of directors at the imposing Mellon Bank, underwriter of Westinghouse Electric and US Steel. Such was his stature in American industry that July 1 marked the two-year-anniversary launch of a massive Great Lakes freighter named in his honor. While Schoonmaker spoke in the Great Tent and its impressive length of 450

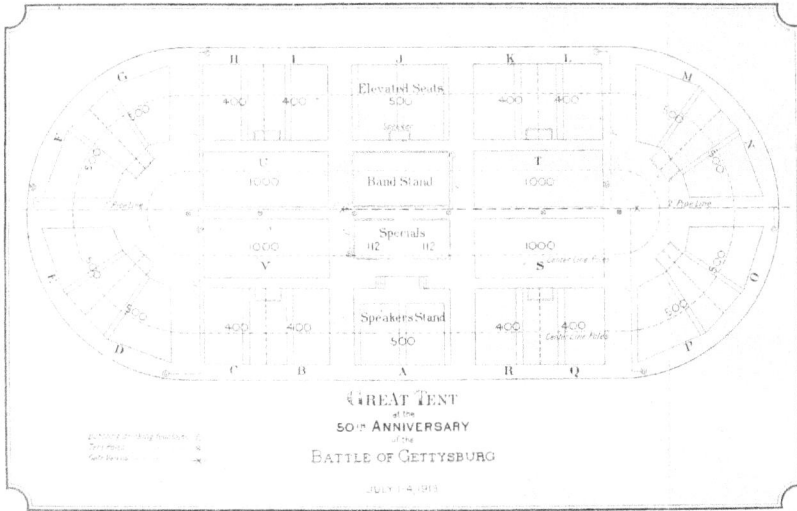

Layout and seating capacities of the Great Tent. At times, sections were subdivided by large curtains, allowing for smaller reunions to be held simultaneously. (*Fiftieth Anniversary of the Battle of Gettysburg: Report of the Pennsylvania Commission*)

feet, the *Schoonmaker* reigned as the largest freshwater vessel in the United States, a stunning 615 feet from bow to stern. Accordingly, the man spoke in grandiose terms. He declared the Reunion officially open and deemed it "a celebration unparalleled in the history of the world." He also heralded Gettysburg as "a battle in which the mortality was greater than in any other recorded in history."[30]

Whether Schoonmaker's statements were accurate (and the latter certainly wasn't) mattered little to him. His intent was to christen the event with reverence and to establish a sense of awe. In turn, he exalted the Reunion as proof of American exceptionalism. For Schoonmaker, a veteran officer of the Army of the Potomac, military operations were not just an obligation for his generation: they were the fate of a vast future also. Promoting a kind of religious nationalism, he contended that to fight other humans was to earn heavenly favor:

Our lives, my comrades, were mercifully spared to see the son of the old soldier of the North stand shoulder to shoulder with the son of the old soldier of the South, and under the leadership of the Generals of the South and the North, sweep San Juan Hill, sink the Spanish fleets in Santiago and Manila Bays, and thundering at the gates of Pekin, establish our country as [a] power second to none on earth. It is eminently fitting, therefore, that with hearts teeming full of gratitude to Almighty God for his goodness and mercy to us, that we should look to Him for blessing and protecting care over us during these intensely interesting exercises.[31]

In keeping with the message of Americans as crusaders, Schoonmaker and his fellow organizers then led the ensuing speeches, as they would every day thereafter, with benedictions. First up was Rev. George Lovejoy, chaplain-in-chief of the Grand Army of the Republic, who encouraged the audience to consider removing their shoes, "for the place whereon we stand is holy ground. Holy indeed, because of the precious blood shed upon these hill slopes and in these vales." Lovejoy continued to praise "the sacrifices of the generous, the blood of the heroic," and though he deviated from Schoonmaker by hoping a universal peace would someday prevail, the pastor insisted that peace would come once all the world would be made Christian.[32]

Then came the keynote, from secretary of war Lindley Garrison, who proceeded to say what he believed the veterans present wanted to hear: "Fifty years ago today, there began here one of those conflicts between man and man, marked by such exhibitions of valor, courage, and almost superhuman endurance as to engrave itself upon the tablet of history. . . . Equal met equal, and in the domain of physical prowess all were worthy of medals of honor. . . . So long as men love valor and worship heroes, the name of Gettysburg, and of those who fought there, will be ever on their lips."[33]

Though moderately well received, Garrison's words were unoriginal in their hyperbole. Social convention, especially at a reunion of this magnitude, almost mandated such an emphasis on combat as manhood. Yet such an address, whether intentionally or otherwise, denied veterans agency. They were not humans, according to Garrison, but gods of war deserving worship. They were flawless, "the men on each side were actuated by high, pure purposes." Directly, the war secretary confirmed their role as messiahs, "the great conflagration, which it was feared would consume our country, merely served to weld the different parts of it so firmly together and into such a perfect whole, that no power can ever break it."[34]

The speeches thereafter followed suit, touting narratives of mass martyrdom and the consecration of a homogeneous United States. From center stage, GAR commander in chief Alfred Beers professed that all veterans present had come "for the honor and glory of their land . . . to recall the valorous deeds which will go down the aisles of time as the most heroic of ancient or modern warfare." His Confederate counterpart Bennett Young added that the Confederacy as well had been sanctified by the blood of men present and past: "The Confederate comes here with his heart still loyal to the South and to those who made the four years of the Confederate nation's life resplendent with heroism, glory, and noblest sacrifice."[35]

Despite their self-styled sanctity, the orations had minimal impact, partly due to poor acoustics. The lack of amplification, the stir of the audience, and the incessant automobile and cart traffic along the adjacent Emmitsburg Road reduced much of the verbosity to a murmur. More significantly, most Reunion-goers never heard any of the major speeches. On this first official day, a journalist from Indiana estimated there were ten times the number of veterans at the National Cemetery than were present in the Great Tent. "All day the stream toward the cemetery continued," he observed, "and those who reached Cemetery Hill spent nearly the whole day there, searching among the graves for their dead comrades, looking for 'Hank's brother from our town,' and for 'Bill, a schoolmate of mine, who fell in my company.'" As for the official program, the Hoosier considered it little more than an exercise in pomposity. "The big circus tent where governors, generals, judges, bankers, and railroad presidents sat on the stage ready to do honor to the veterans by reciting their deeds of valor and glory, was largely ignored by the honored guests, the old soldiers. The graves of 'Bill' and 'Hank's brother' and 'Jake' were much closer to their hearts."[36] Another writer observed how the higher echelons physically and visually separated themselves from the masses: "The most gorgeous party was the staffs of the visiting governors and the United States army officers, particularly those in white, with their wealth of gold lace and insignia, and their dangling swords. . . . These high officials had their cool quarters at the Lutheran Seminary, apart from the common rank and file, who sweltered on the 'old camp ground.'"[37]

Of those who heard and read the orations, many found the rhetoric less than convincing, particularly when compared to what the veterans were saying to each other. As the *Harrisburg Telegraph* shared with its readers, "Heroism is blasted. It is a delusion and a snare. Around every campfire every night the great part of the talk is about fear." A man from Pickett's Division concurred, saying of his fellow veterans, "If he said he wasn't afraid, the truth is not in him." Luther Ferris of the 179th New York admitted, "I dodged, and here I am. Every man dodges, and if he says he doesn't, he's a braggart." James Vernon of Keyser, West Virginia, admitted that he went no farther than the sight of the Bloody Angle on the battle's third day. Marching into the fray with the 18th Virginia, he acknowledged, "I looked at the stone wall and, seeing the Yankee battle line, I thought it was time for me to get out, and out I got . . . and I kept on going." By his own account, Vernon had been shaken before the charge commenced. During the artillery barrage, he took refuge under an ambulance stretcher with three other companions, and then a shell exploded above them. Shrapnel ripped the back of Vernon's uniform and killed the men with whom he was sitting. Such confessions evidently had a widely relieving effect, a fact recognized by many civilian witnesses. One observer said of the old men, "the happiest hours of their lives were spent in town or on the field meeting old and new friends and talking over the stirring times off fifty years ago. That was their chief delight—of far more pleasure than attending exercises and listening to speeches."[38]

Nor was the official band particularly popular. One of the more common and playful pursuits among the veterans involved creating their own music. Civilian Earl Godwin said of the encampment, "If there is one odd feature to be remembered here, it is the remarkable number of fifers, drummers, and a slightly less number of buglers of all ages, from sixty-five years to eighty." From the first arrivals, instrumentals and sing-alongs sprouted like wildflowers. "Dixie" and "Battle Cry of Freedom" were perennials, though the week's repertoire covered a wide array. From martial pieces to love songs, from the melancholic to the goofy, players and listeners alike marveled at how the melodies made them feel years younger. Well before sunup and far past sundown, the town, streets, and tent rows hummed with renditions of "Arkansas Traveler," "Turkey in the Straw," "Johnny Comes Marching Home," and "The Streets of Cairo." Players usually congregated into small intimate groups, but occasionally they spontaneously formed grand parades. Significantly, many of the bugles, drums, fiddles, and fifes were used in the war. Such personal ar-

One of many im-
promptu music
sessions at the en-
campment, which
commonly included
instruments that the
players used in the war.
Also note the hatband
worn by the gentleman
on the right. Vendors
sold countless such
souvenirs to attendees,
who wore them mostly
to find and be found by
others from their home
state. (Courtesy Harris
and Ewing Collection,
Library of Congress)

tifacts, and their familiar sound, established audible connections to the
past and provided the ability to compose a new present.[39]

If there was one universal joy in the camp that surpassed even music,
it was the abundance and variety of food. "Gosh ain't this great feed?" ex-
claimed a veteran from Vermont. "Some different than what we had fifty
years ago. Then it was hard tack and sow belly, and not half enough at
that."[40] By July 1 it was clear that the succulent fare was going to be standard practice. "We were fed the best food obtainable," said James Hall
of Texas, "and it was prepared in fine style. Every arrangement for our
comfort was made."[41]

For lunch on July 1, Fickas and his mates feasted on fresh bread and
butter, coffee, iced tea, milk, roast beef, roast potatoes, mashed turnips,
and a dessert of rice pudding. The whole affair came compliments of
173 kitchens and 425 army field ranges, operated by two thousand cooks

and assistants. The enormous commissary cache for the week included 7,000 cans of fish, 9,000 pounds of salt, 12,000 pounds of coffee, 60,000 pounds of sugar, 130,000 pounds of flour, 156,410 pounds of red meat, 216,777 pounds of fresh vegetables, and nearly 300,000 eggs.[42]

Veterans at mess. Altogether, organizers provided over 168,000 meals per day. (Courtesy George Grantham Bain Collection, Library of Congress)

One of two long rows of kitchens that served the massive Pennsylvania section of camp just south of town. Visible here are about 20 percent of the kitchens for that one state alone. Note the electrical, telephone, and telegraph wires overhead, modern conveniences that kept the veterans connected and cared for. (Courtesy George Grantham Bain Collection, Library of Congress)

Army stoves made for hot work in the kitchens, which only added to the praise these cooks and bakers received from their grateful clientele. (Courtesy George Grantham Bain Collection, Library of Congress)

Compare this to the Gettysburg campaign. For Waldron and his men, one of their primary motives for the long march northward was to gather grain and livestock for an emaciated Virginia. During the battle, Daniel Krebs of the 1st Maryland Infantry tried to survive on one hardtack cracker per day. Union soldiers recalled stealing honey from hives and onions from local families. As a farmer during most of the war, H. H. Hodges was generally aware that his county—and in fact the Confederacy—produced surplus amounts of food. Widespread hunger came from the breakdown of transportation systems. At the Reunion, he saw wagons, automobiles, and refrigerated railcars brimming with foodstuffs. At the end of every street stood the kitchens and bakeries. Each morning the men awoke to the smell of fresh bread and brewing coffee wafting into their tents. The hungriest would grab their mess kits and gain a prime spot at the front of the line. For the early birds and late risers alike, the food was a gift, as was the liberating feeling that they did not serve the army anymore. The army served them.[43]

Food was not the only benefit the War Department delivered. Alerted to the unforeseen overflow of attendees, the army transported in an

The camp bakeries managed to turn out cakes, pies, pastries, and small moun-
tains of fresh bread, consuming 130,048 pounds of flour and several tons of butter, eggs, fruit, salt, and sugar in the process. (Courtesy Library of Congress)

additional twenty-eight thousand blankets and eight thousand mattresses on July 1. The veterans also assisted when and where they could,
taking in stragglers who had lost their way or whose state encampments
had become overpopulated. As one person noted, while witnessing the
repeated acts of empathy, "Confederates sheltered Yankees, and Yankees
harbored their one-time foes."[44]

Such experiences made it possible for attendees to simply enjoy themselves and feel welcomed. The stimuli of the day's events could also trigger intense emotions, including elation. Back in July 1, 1863, Company
A of the 20th North Carolina had lost half its flag when it was ripped
from its mast during the battle. Fifty years later, one H. M. Fitzgerald of
a New York regiment wandered into the North Carolina section of camp
and asked where the company might be. He then proceeded to tell them
that he had the missing half and wanted to return it, which prompted a
virtual party that lasted well into the night.[45]

CHAPTER 6

"Military Day"

"We hustled pell-mell over the fields, every fellow bent on finding the numerous locations that held the greatest interest. For hours we thus wandered over those fascinating fields, stopping here and there to point out just where a certain comrade fell or where the speaker himself was wounded. It was a weird spectacle; those aged veterans wandering over the hills where the horrors of death once hovered. . . . After tiring ourselves out in tramping we again repaired to our tents for refreshment. . . . every day a repetition of the one preceding."
—Elijah Boland, 13th Alabama

Boland's testimony reflected how place and relationships, more than clock and calendar, infused meaning. Rhode Island's official report confirmed this tendency among its own veterans: "the exercises in the great tent were interesting, impressive, and well attended, but there seemed to be more pleasure for the majority in wandering over the battlefield or visiting about the camp."[1]

This July 2, A. C. Smith of the 56th Virginia cared little that he was a day early for the fiftieth anniversary of Pickett's Charge. He simply wanted to see the Angle again. Once he reached the wall, Smith relayed how "here I fell the day of Pickett's Charge and some Union man came 'long an' picked me up an' saved my life." Albert M. Hamilton of the 72nd Pennsylvania stood a few feet away recalling how he gave water to a wounded rebel and carried him to an aid station. Upon hearing Hamilton's account,

Smith walked over, held him by the shoulder and looked into his face. After a few moments, Smith said, "Why, good god, mister. You're the man who saved my life!" Taken aback, Hamilton paused, and he, too, believed (or wanted to believe) the reconnection was real. Witnesses patted the men on their shoulders, and the pair walked away arm in arm. As Heman Allen's fellow Vermonter Richard Wright said, "It was not unusual to see veterans of both the Blue and the Gray clasped in each other's arms and weeping as they met for the first time in 50 years."[2] Equally as moving was the discovery of a long-lost comrade. Remi Boerner of Philadelphia was walking downtown when someone embraced him from behind. Boerner turned to see that it was an old friend from his regiment, the 91st Pennsylvania. The two had not seen each other since being discharged in 1865.[3]

A frequent means of preserving these memories, and commemorating survivorship, involved photography. In high demand were professional portrait makers, who wisely descended upon the scene, such as Philip Myers and his friend Russ Lewis. The two secured a prime spot at Devil's Den and soon found themselves wonderfully inundated with customers wanting a snapshot in front of the iconic boulders. "The pile of exposed plates rose prodigiously," Myers recalled, "making a backlog of developing and printing that took months to clear."[4] A commercial breakthrough from the Eastman Kodak Company helped democratize the process of recording history when in 1900 the rudimentary "Brownie" became available for a modest $1. By 1913 there were several hundred thousand sold, and an untold number made their way to the Reunion.

As during the war itself, citizen-soldiers at the Reunion preferred to give and receive individual portraits. At Vermont's popular Tent Number 4, Heman Allen and friends cared for a Virginian in need. Moved by their kindness and generosity, the old Johnny asked how he could ever repay them. They responded that all would be square if he gave them his picture. The following morning, the visitor returned with his image in hand.[5]

Such intimate encounters were often overshadowed by a turn-of-the-century innovation: the ability to transfer photos onto the pages of newspapers. Consequently, much of what the public saw of the Jubilee came through selective lenses. At times, the imagery was heavily edited and thoroughly staged. Reporter Robert Gorman called out his colleagues for their manipulations, although their subjects didn't seem concerned: "Thousands upon thousands of old veterans of the North and South have been 'shot' during the past four days. The old soldiers have been made to do foolish things. Too, as they say, for the life of the newspapers of the country. Press photographers have placed them in all kinds of poses, from the now familiar hand shake to a position dancing an old-fashioned jig. But after all they seem to enjoy their experiences. . . . All is merry in the camp and the veterans are ever willing to comply with any requests made by a photographer."[6]

In her examination of Kodak's early history, Nancy Martha West finds that the ubiquity of personal cameras by the early twentieth century created a commitment to nostalgia among users, as well as a longing among them to exhibit the family as unified and happy. Although photojournalists of the era covered a far broader scope, their treatment of the Jubilee mimicked the emerging social convention. In their newsprint snapshots, newspapermen presented veterans as idealized and harmonious kinfolk.[7] Gorman may have exaggerated the image of dancing vets, but much of the professional *and* amateur camerawork at Gettysburg was choreographed with the consumer in mind. Clasped hands were indeed the standard; faces turned toward the camera; a backdrop of tents, flags, or monuments; and smiles supplanting the traditional Victorian scowl. Common, too, were shots of old boys at play: fifers and drummers stirring a tune, cane-swinging "sword fights," and hikers traversing the rugged landscape.

There was considerable truth to these warm images. Many of the men genuinely expressed joie du vivre. Widespread were sentiments of relief from years of loneliness, the comfort found among kindred spirits, and a sense of belonging otherwise missing in their everyday lives. One of the sincerest demonstrations of this rejuvenation, documented on film countless times, involved the sense of touch. "The favorite pose—I must have made a thousand exposures of it," recalled Philip Myers, "was for a Yank and a Reb to stand with arms intertwined in fraternal amity."[8] Gettysburg survivor Tom Painter attested to the profound impact of physically reconnecting: "There is only one thing that clings in memory more than a handshake, and that's the feel of the shoulder hunch that your comrade gave you when you were close in ranks. After fifty years the soldier feels yet that hunch of the shoulder. It feels good in memory. It reminds him now, as it told him then, of the comrade close at his side—the real comrade, the man with whom he had bunked and with whom he had shared his rations." This chance to once again give and receive human contact,

Outsiders frequently interpreted physical contact between old foes as the resolution of sectional discord. In reality, veterans were expressing their fundamental need for human contact. Handshakes and embraces helped attendees to communicate a sense of mutual understanding and compassion. (Courtesy Pennsylvania Historical and Museum Commission, Pennsylvania State Archives, RG 25.24, Records of Special Commissions, Fiftieth Anniversary of the Battle of Gettysburg)

Painter believed, was the most valuable part of the Reunion. By embracing each other, veterans could show and receive compassion, confirming their survivorship. "In a sense we are all fighting in a battle," he said, "it is the world-old battle for life and perhaps for the means of living."9

Frequently, these intimate scenes were altered for the purposes of mythmaking and political gain. Among the most commonly published images were of government officials posing with a select few in blue and gray. One of the more conspicuous uses of the men as props transpired outside the Gettysburg Hotel on July 2, where Pennsylvania congressman A. J. Barchfeld repeatedly nabbed passersby for his own promotion. "He stands in front of the hostelry all day," observed a local journalist, "and 'collars' Union and Confederate veterans as they appear and has them pose for pictures with himself as the central attraction. He says he expects to use the pictures in his next campaign."[10] A common sight on front pages was pictures of dignitaries like war secretary Lindley Garrison and Pennsylvania governor John Tener smiling approvingly over their contented wards.

Back in the Great Tent, the rhetoric continued to place greater emphasis on death. On July 2, no speaker articulated this theme with greater zeal than Gov. Samuel Ralston. The rotund, mustachioed Ralston had risen from the Indiana coal mines to the executive office of the Hoosier State, partly from diligent study of law and partly from the state's Democratic machinery. A conservative Presbyterian at home, he delivered a sermon at Gettysburg worthy of a revivalist. If persons were to consider themselves true patriots, Ralston told his audience, they must acknowledge the Battle of Gettysburg as a noble mass martyrdom for the salvation of all Americans. When a person accepted the terrible battle as instead a national blessing, Ralston claimed, "the American Republic, made indissoluble by American blood, shall be the beginning of his joy, the renewing of his faith, and the strengthening of his devotion." He thanked the veterans for "that supreme test of manhood—devotion to duty unto death," and concluded by reassuring them that they would soon be joining their dead brethren. "With security you can walk down the short and shortening path of life, as the curtain lowers about you." It is unlikely that veterans in attendance found much comfort in Ralston's insistence that they were about to die, nor would they cherish the thought that the ancient Greek word for such a quiet and contented death is *euthanasia*.[11]

By this time the attraction of the Great Tent, with its redundant orations on eternal rest, had run its course. The place was less than half full on July 2, and only about half of that small audience were veterans. The Gettysburg as Golgotha premise may have resonated with some, but most spent the day reassuring themselves that they, and their old foes, were still very much alive.[12] There were still sites to see, band concerts to hear, camaraderie to enjoy, and delicacies to savor. W. B. Prather found the commemoration "all a marvel; it would have to be seen to be appreciated." Some even hoped to fall in love. Weeks before the anniversary, the burgess of Gettysburg received a note from St. James, Missouri, reading, "there are four or five of our old veterans of the battle of Gettysburg who will be in your city at the celebration, and if you have a few good widows or old maids who would like to marry and go West, we can accommodate

A study in contrasts: the festoonery of officers and organizers (*above*) and the reserved garb of citizen-soldiers (*below*). (Courtesy Pennsylvania Historical and Museum Commission, Pennsylvania State Archives, RG 25.24, Records of Special Commissions, Fiftieth Anniversary of the Battle of Gettysburg)

a few. They must be good housekeepers, and not too young."[13] Whether any of the suitors received a rose is unknown, but two old sweethearts did find each other: "John Goodwin, of New York, a veteran, and Mrs. Margaret Murphy, of Chicago, were married this morning by Squire Harnish in his office on Centre Square. Forty-six years ago the two were engaged, but some circumstances prevented their marriage and later each married another. They became widower and widow, the old flame was rekindled and they agreed to come to Gettysburg on the fiftieth anniversary of the battle and remarry."[14]

Out in the fields and hills, regiments continued to hold their own reunions. Members of the 29th Pennsylvania gathered together at Culp's Hill, the place where they helped repulse a nighttime attack. Survivors of the 155th Pennsylvania collected along their old defensive position on Little Round Top. Members of the 62nd Pennsylvania did the same at the Wheatfield. Individuals continued their personal searches. James Hall of the 5th Pennsylvania looked for the spot where he had been wounded in the Peach Orchard. James Vernon of Keyser, West Virginia, spent much time with his old captain Robert McCulloch. The two had not seen each other since the war.[15]

These formal and informal gatherings intrinsically functioned as group therapy. Returning to combat sites like Gettysburg, and doing so in the company of those who went through the same trials, created a safe and supportive environment for those otherwise unable to address their past.[16] Central to this healing process was "the talking cure," an organic act somewhat similar to the late-nineteenth-century work of Viennese physicians Josef Breuer and Sigmund Freud. In pioneering psychoanalysis, Breuer and Freud aimed to be professional, impartial observers, listening to their clients in a neutral setting. By comparison, veterans preferred small groups, consisting almost exclusively of people who endured the same struggles in the same locations.[17] Conducive to this bonding was their shared language. Place names, military terms, and soldier slang formed a common vocabulary. This vernacular was evidently preferable to the romanticized prose that persisted in the Great Tent, which helps explain why a journalist observed on July 2, "Comparatively few veterans appeared to listen to the speechmaking."[18]

Prevalent was the desire to piece together a more cohesive image of what they saw and heard. Contrary to public orations depicting combat

as orderly, heroic displays, personal memories tended to be far more dis-
turbed and fragmented. Sitting and speaking with fellow survivors helped
many weave together a clearer picture of chaotic events. The search did
not always bring peace. For those who could not find comrades or opponents who underwent the same ordeals, memories often remained unre-
solved. Disagreements on how far a given company advanced, or which
unit was first to run, led to many emotionally charged exchanges. Yet predominantly the effect of sharing stories transcended assumed alliances.
A local journalist remarked how diverse these small circles could be, including one "being a mixture of socialist, agnostic, and Sunday school
superintendent."[19] For veterans who viewed themselves alone with their
traumatic past, enjoining others in the same emotional state often felt
reassuring, and at times euphoric. As one Gettysburg resident observed,
"at various places about the camp some veteran will start a war-time song
and others with join in; others have brought along games and enjoy their
periods of rest with a social time in the tent. . . . From reveille to taps the
veterans enjoy themselves, while some of them do not retire with taps,
preferring to spend much of the night in talking." Another saw how "the
old soldiers by twos and threes found each other, and in camp or on the
field they spent hours talking."[20]

Though veterans often showed marginal connection to what the government was saying about mortal combat in 1863, the men showed sincere gratitude for what the government was doing to keep them healthy
in 1913. In theory, the Jubilee was supposed to glorify a mythic past;
in practice, it reflected modern progressivism, and the old-timers were
widely grateful for it. The plethora of accommodations convinced many
citizen-soldiers that their government had matured since the war, from
a frequently inefficient military operator into an efficacious public utility.
Nearly universal was the praise for the medical care, fresh water, assistance from the Boy Scouts and US Army, and even the tent accommodations. Noticed also was the absence of a wartime camp's sickening traits:
diseases, putrid smells, and proliferating insects. As one person bragged,
"Not a single case of typhoid has developed. Flies are scarce. Major Hut-
ten [director of the Medical Corps] defies anybody to find an odor in the
camp."[21] As one man summarized, "the total number of deaths [at the
Reunion] was less than that sustained by many a company that fought
in the great battle."[22]

Appreciated, too, was another service rarely experienced in soldier life: an abundance of information. Knowledgeable guides, clearly marked signs and streets, information kiosks, and eighty-seven army telephones linked by ninety miles of wiring all kept the veterans well connected. In the center of camp stood the temporary post office; each day an estimated fifty thousand postcards passed through its half-dozen windows. Altogether the modest, wood-frame structure handled more than a half-million pieces of mail. Tourists also sent postcards, bearing the station's unique stamp. In return came letters from home, which were received with the same joy as when the men were young. Enormously plentiful were newspapers: the *New York Times, Philadelphia Inquirer, Washington Herald,* and scores of others. Some twenty-five thousand newspapers were sold on-site each day. The *Harrisburg Telegraph* boasted six thousand copies sold on July 2 alone, a distribution said to be "the largest in the history of the paper." Regional papers trucked in their print by train and automobile, distributed by a small army of newsboys. During the war, soldiers often waited weeks for news. At the anniversary, the *Harrisburg Telegraph* bragged about how it could deliver its latest edition to the battlefield in two hours, via a forty-horsepower, five-passenger "Oakland" from the Harrisburg Automobile Company. Every evening, the car would return with glass negatives and film from field photographers, and every following afternoon it would return with piles of papers and more newsies, with eager buyers seeing if their likeness and interviews made it into print. In turn, the camp's 155 journalists kept the country attuned to the veterans' well-being. Heman Allen's son could read about him in the *Burlington Free Press,* as could William Fickas's family in Phoenix's *Arizona Republic.*[23]

Clearly the most cherished information involved what veterans shared on the battleground and around the campfire, details and perspectives that helped address the aching gaps. Yet for a large portion of the attendees, the Gettysburg Reunion was just that—a reunion of, by, and for Gettysburg veterans. The reductionism had an alienating effect. For veterans of the Western Theater (where the majority of Americans resided, and most of the war's battles took place), there emerged a growing sense of marginalization, and their numbers at the Reunion were not small. Of twenty-five men in and around Houston who attended, eighteen were not veterans of Gettysburg, nor were forty-four of the sixty-five men who left from Salt Lake City. As large as it was, the Battle of Gettysburg involved

Many veterans brought with them personal relics of their time in the war, to show to others and themselves physical proof of their participation and to extract memories of their wartime experiences. (Courtesy George Grantham Bain Collection, Library of Congress)

less than 9 percent of all men who ever fought for the Confederacy and less than 5 percent who served in the Union. Federal veterans of the Western Theater especially had reasons to wonder why the Army of the Potomac, which took four years to advance across a portion of Virginia, deserved the highest of accolades, when the Armies of the Cumberland, the Mississippi, the Ohio, and others managed to sweep from Arkansas to the Carolinas over the same period. As a columnist for the *New York Times* noticed, "The man who can merely say that he was at Shiloh with Grant or was one of those who dashed back the tide that rushed upon the Rock of Chickamauga has somewhat the feeling of a guest."[24]

For these outsiders, encounters with old friend and foes were still possible. W. H. McLeod had been a captive in the infamous Camp Douglas POW compound in Chicago. During the Reunion he met an ex-Federal soldier who served as a guard there. The two men bonded over how neither wanted to be at the prison. McLeod returned home with a badge given to him by his old captor, a tangible reminder of their finding each other.[25]

Overlooked more so were veterans of the navies. Six of Vermont's cadre had served in the navy, as did thirteen in the Rhode Island camp and scores among the New Yorkers and Pennsylvanians. William Durst, a Philadelphian, was reportedly the last surviving member of the USS *Monitor.* Dressed in his old uniform in hopes of meeting more of his sailing veterans, he quickly became disappointed. "These fellows insist on talking about charges and camps and all that sort of thing," he lamented. "Not one of them knows a thing about sailing. I guess I'll go back home." One reporter said of him, "Durst wanders around like a lost sheep."[26]

In this largest-ever Civil War Reunion, individuals could still feel alone and abandoned. An Ohio journalist reported, "Two veterans have been found in camp apparently without friends, who are totally blind, and they are quartered in hospital tents." Others were greatly limited by sudden exhaustion, acute illness, or lingering injuries. One of the most common and isolating preexisting conditions involved severe hearing loss, which limited the opportunity to partake in the talking cure. Mississippian Frank H. Foote estimated that two out of every five men he met in camp were "afflicted with deafness." His calculation may have been close to accurate. Years after the war, around one-third of Union pensioners were diagnosed with significant hearing loss. Artillerists like Fickas were most vulnerable, exposed as they were time and again to their instruments' concussive blasts. Nearly as susceptible to eardrum damage, and in far greater numbers, were infantrymen like Hodges and Waldron. The countless cracks of their own weapons turned them into silent casualties.[27]

Even those who were at the battle could perceive themselves as outsiders, especially when organizers emphasized combat as Gettysburg's defining attribute. W. M. Akers of the 6th Virginia felt as if he missed the fight, being held in reserve to guard artillery units. As a result, Akers declined to attend. Then there were individuals like Dillard C. Howell of Virginia, who had been drafted into the Confederate Army, very much against his wishes. He and his company in the 24th Virginia played a central role in Pickett's deadly foray, but he could not bring himself to make the trip again. Almost anyone from the Union's 6th Corps might feel like a minor character in this great retelling, as nearly the entirety of that unit's fourteen thousand men were held in reserve.[28]

Almost totally absent were African American veterans. By the end of the war, they constituted one in ten Union service members. At the

Reunion, the ratio was closer to one in a thousand. Manifold are the reasons for the disparity. Life spans had some effect. Subjected to greater levels of poverty and less access to healthcare, African American males in the 1910s had a life expectancy in the mid-thirties compared to the low-fifties for their white counterparts. Also, much of the press collectively overlooked USCT participation. The *Harrisburg Telegraph* reported how "most of the State delegations in the Union camp have several posts of colored representatives, and of course there are many, many stories the gray-haired negro fighters can tell," yet editors neglected to print those stories. The *Telegraph* itself heralded attendee Ephraim Hopple as a former slave who bravely escaped bondage to serve in the Union army, but the paper added nothing more about his service or his experiences at the Reunion.[29]

Arguably the primary reason for underrepresentation involved self-exclusion. While the Anniversary Commission warmly and overtly invited ex-Confederates (including the allowance of Confederate uniforms and battle flags), they offered no direct overtures to veterans of color. Nor were there any minorities on any federal or state committee involved in organizing the event. In addition, nearly 90 percent of African American citizens still lived in the South. For southern-based veterans, the prospect of riding on segregated trains, without financial support, connected to carloads of former Confederates would have been a potentially unsettling proposition at best. At the commemoration, the advertised schedule of speakers included neither African Americans nor veterans of the USCT. Orators slated to attend included multiple ex-Confederate officers, the first southern-born president elected since the Civil War, and the chief justice of the United States Supreme Court, who, as an associate justice, ruled in favor of racial segregation in *Plessy v. Ferguson*.

There certainly was a strong African American presence, albeit mostly in the form of cooks and kitchen assistants. J. R. Fix of Kansas observed that former Confederates predominantly had white cooks while the old Union men generally had African Americans in their kitchens. His hometown paper snidely remarked that it was because "each wanted a change when they went away from home."[30]

As for minority veterans, Walter Blake of New Jersey witnessed how some could be treated. "A giant of an old negro, Samuel Thompson, from Mount Holly, was resting under some shade trees, when along came a crowd of old Confederates." Blake recalled how they approached Thompson and said, "We all are glad to see you, and we all want to shake hands with you, nigger, and to say as we have some niggers at home just as big as you." Blake added, "Every one of the Southerners stepped up and followed the example of their comrade, shaking hands with their dark-skinned brother, and slapping him with a kindly slap."[31]

An afternoon rainstorm received a sincerer welcome. The bright lightning and clapping thunder startled some, but much like the talking sessions and revisits to old sites, the rainfall brought temperate relief. Reflecting the calming atmosphere, just as the official events were ramping up, the attendance was dropping off. The Jubilee reached its peak visitation sometime during the afternoon. By that point, veterans either found what they were seeking or had become dejected in the attempt. Gen. Hunter Liggett conservatively estimated that by midnight, somewhere between five thousand and six thousand veterans had already departed.[32] A few left wondering if the great assembly would ever produce a second Gettysburg Address, but no such opus arose from the patter. The doggerel verbosity from the Great Tent led one observer to jest: "Speaking of that Gettysburg reunion." "Yes?" "What a lot of good feeling it did cause." "And what a lot of bad poetry."[33]

Across the encampment, Waldron and others opted to write their own verse. Their most prolific hours were after sundown, when the relative serenity allowed time for letter writing and long conversations. Many commented how nightfall turned the Reunion quietly beautiful. Walter Blake looked down from a knoll and marveled at all the visiting taking place, as "lanterns flashed in and out among the tents; in the distance they looked like hundreds of fireflies flitting about."[34] Part of the calming effect came from the greenish lamplights of aid stations and rows of golden streetlights. From the vantage of Cemetery Ridge, Frank Kenfield expressed, "At night the grandeur and beauty of this camp was beyond description. Lighted by electricity, it presented a scene, to those who saw it, that will ever be remembered."[35]

If the Reunion established peace, it came to individuals by ones and twos. Among the general populace, underlying animosities endured. A potent reminder erupted around 6:30 P.M. that night in the downtown Gettysburg Hotel. In a crowded dining room, a Union veteran took offense at a derogatory remark about Abraham Lincoln. The alleged source of the insult was one William Byrd Henry, the son of a former Confederate officer. In response, the old soldier threw a water tumbler at Mr. Henry, who then chased the aged veteran with a knife and started stabbing those in his way. Among eight injured were a member of the US Army, an African American who worked at the hotel, and a state trooper. The most seriously hurt was civilian Charles Ensor, who was stabbed six times, including four times in the back. When apprehended, the knife-wielding Henry denied any wrongdoing.[36]

Rushing to Henry's defense was his prominent Virginia family. Soon to follow were Virginia governor William Hodges Mann, Lt. Gov. Gen. James Taylor Ellyson, and Attorney Gen. Samuel Walker Williams, all of whom were former Confederate officers. They quickly pooled enough money to secure Henry's bond of $2,500 (approximately $61,000 in 2018) and publicly voiced an assurance that Henry came from highly reputable stock.[37]

All but one of the stabbing victims eventually filed lawsuits. Before the year was out, a judge dismissed every case, ruling that the perpetrator had been "laboring under a temporary mental aberration," adding, "Mr. Henry, you are not before the court as a criminal. You are here as a victim of circumstances."[38]

Though extreme, the above altercation was not an isolated incident. The Reunion itself saw eight additional assaults that required hospitalization, tensions over national flags, verbal altercations, and multiple examples during which veterans could forgive each other but not the actions of their wartime governments. Despite having made some social and economic advances since the war, the nation still suffered from intrinsic divisions that could not be assuaged by a single weeklong commemoration.[39]

CHAPTER 7

"Governors' Day"

"Those who were not there can form no idea of it."
—James Vernon, 18th Virginia, July 3, 1913

The organizers could have selected a more appropriate name for the day, but at least they remained committed to their theme: the speaker lineup at the Great Tent featured ten governors. Also scheduled were the US House of Representative chaplain, vice president Thomas Marshall, and Speaker of the House Champ Clark. The audience was the smallest yet, with the tent less than half full. Notably Heman Allen, William Fickas, H. H. Hodges, and Moses Waldron never mentioned attending any event at the main tent.[1]

From the rostrum came more adulation of sacrifice and death. In a brief and pious oration, Champ Clark employed the word "valor" no fewer than eleven times. Gov. William Sulzer of New York added, "The intervening years have only added greater splendor to the sacrifice sublime, and a grander glory to the victory triumphant." Sectionalism also crept into the speeches. First among the governors was James McCreary of Kentucky, a Confederate veteran, who lectured at length about the substantial Confederate presence in the existing US government, including chief justice Edward White, associate justice Horace Lurton, former war secretary Jacob Dickerson, and himself. McCreary also proclaimed that the war "demonstrated the states have rights that must be respected." At least Minnesota governor Adolph Eberhart kept a sense of humor over the proceedings. He told the patient veterans in the audience, "What an indescribable pleasure must be experienced by Vice President Marshall, who presides over the Senate, and Speaker Clark, who presides over the House, to come here and look into the faces of so many honest men."[2]

Last up was Pennsylvania governor John Tener. Leading the Pennsylvania Commission since his inauguration in 1911, having procured nearly a half-million dollars in funding (more than all other states combined), playing the role of moderate between Union and Confederate sympathies, Tener had a vested interest in painting the Reunion as one of national reconciliation. While not as effusive as others on themes of death and martyrdom, he did subscribe to their consistent directive to forget the past. As others had done before him, Tener insisted, "The wounds are healed . . . the bitterness is gone, past differences are settled."[3] The basic message was that it was patriotic to forget one's own history. John H. Leathers, a sergeant major in the Stonewall Brigade, implored from the rostrum, "Nobody need now discuss the past. The men of the Confederacy have their faces turned toward the future." On July 1, in his opening prayer, GAR chaplain-in-chief George Lovejoy suggested, "All that has been painful in our past we would forget in our holier, happier impulses of the present." Secretary of war Lindley Garrison concurred: "This meeting is the final demonstration that the last embers of the former time have been stamped out."[4]

Amid these erasure attempts came a more candid assessment. Roswell Burchard, lieutenant governor of Rhode Island, may have listened with unease to such statements. When his time came to speak, Burchard warned, "It is a false and insincere sentiment that would ask us to forget and entirely forgive the calamities of the war. Brothers cannot forget the death of brothers, nor can mothers forgive the slaughter of sons."[5]

One of the most pointed disconnects between what veterans did and what officials said involved the act of remembering. For veterans, returning to combat sites like Gettysburg naturally created resurgence rather than repression of memory. As the Reunion showed time and again, many survivors demonstrated a desire to address their past experiences in spite of (and often because of) the traumatic or profound nature of such experiences. This human impulse to retrieve memory is a central reason why the veterans generally bypassed official speeches; there was much to retrace elsewhere. Even then, organizers tried to frame the past into a more ideal-

Daniel Sickles arrives by motor car to the ceremony of Pickett's Charge. Despite the legacy of the Confederate assault on July 3, Sickles continued to proclaim that it was his defense of the Peach Orchard and Wheatfield salient on July 2 that decided the battle and "saved the Union." (Courtesy George Grantham Bain Collection, Library of Congress)

ized image. Nowhere was this done more conspicuously than on the hour anniversary of Pickett's Charge, an official event scheduled for 3:00 P.M.

Around thirty minutes before, while the speeches in the Great Tent were under way, a small crowd began to form around the Bloody Angle. Within minutes it became a sea of people, a flowing mass dotted with cream-white skimmers and pitch-black umbrellas. A young man in attendance remembered feeling overwhelmed, as "thousands, and still other thousands of spectators filled every available vantage point and were kept from spilling over the limiting markers only by the fixed bayonets of the Regulars. A feeling of tense excitement swept through the huge throng."[6] Churning the waters, a gaggle of automobiles puttered and plodded about, searching for a prime spot from which to watch the proceedings. VIP passengers included Maj. Gen. Daniel Sickles and ninety-year-old Edwin Berkeley of the 8th Virginia, the latter being the

Members of the 72nd Pennsylvania wait in the heat for formal events to begin at the Bloody Angle. (Courtesy George Grantham Bain Collection, Library of Congress)

oldest survivor from Pickett's ranks. Upon seeing the deluge of sightseers and motor carriages, Berkeley asked, "We didn't have that much confusion fifty years ago, did we?"[7]

The same thought may have entered the minds of the Philadelphia Brigade members as they assembled just north of the Angle. They were instructed to walk as a group and retake the very positions they held during the charge. Reports varied as to how many survivors were present. Estimates ranged from 120 to 300. Among them was William Fickas's travel companion Andrew Weaber, who had traveled all the way from Arizona to relive this moment. As the top of the hour approached, Weaber and his companions filed forth, into the packed assembly, wedging their way between the onlookers and the east side of the low stone wall.[8]

About five hundred yards to their west, around 120 survivors of Pickett's Division collected in the Confederate side of camp, less than 1 percent of the entire line that went forward in 1863. Representing the 28th Virginia, Moses Waldron and William Gooley waited patiently for the signal to move out. In 1863 the 28th went in with approximately 235 officers and men, including Waldron's uncle John and his tentmate Thomas McDaniel. That day there were perhaps a half dozen left. Among them

was their old lieutenant, Thomas Holland; former private, Calvin Dearing; and Phillip Aliff, who had lost an arm in this very attack.[9]

The companionship likely helped. Each man was about to retrace the
same path he took as part of Lee's lead wave, heading straight for a point
between a stone wall and a clump of trees. Emotionally, physically, this
was going to be a difficult walk. Today, they were under the direction
of Maj. W. W. Bentley of the 24th Virginia, whose regiment started the
assault several hundred yards to the right of Waldron's. There would be
no distance between them this day; their numbers were far too few. At
the time of the battle, their mutual commanding officer was Brig. Gen.
Richard Garnett, who against the advice of fellow officers, went into the
engagement mounted on his horse. Garnett and his animal made a large
and easy target for the artillery unit directly to their front, Lt. Alonzo
Cushing's Battery A.

When the organizers were satisfied that all was ready, Major Bentley
gave the order to proceed. Waldron, Gooley, Dearing, and their associates
eventually formed a long meandering column, with the Kesnech's Mu-
nicipal Band of Richmond leading the way, playing "Dixie" over and over.
Midway down the line, a Confederate national flag waved aloft. A reporter
from the *New York Tribune* watched as the men slowly made their way
across the train tracks and filed through the Connecticut and Michigan
sections of camp. "Some of them carried their coats on their arms, some
walked with sticks and others under umbrellas, for it was infernally hot.
As they straggled by the Union tents, the old boys in blue poured forth to
delay them by shaking them by the hand and patting them on the back."
Waldron and company pressed through waist-high timothy, shakily trying to keep their balance over rutted ground and dense grass. A witness
simply described the procession as "slow and painful."[10]

Watching them approach, George Goodlander from the 72nd Pennsylvania thought, "We went over the field and received again the charge of
Pickett's men at Bloody Angle. Fifty years ago it took them twenty minutes to make that charge, but [now] it took an hour and a half. . . . Fifty
years ago I was wondering if I could get away." Watching his counterparts
struggle during this reenactment, Goodlander admitted, "I was wondering if the veterans could get up there."[11]

Waldron began to think back to the screeching Federal ordnance and
how it plowed through his friends. While crossing Emmitsburg Road,

Gooley may have felt compelled to stop. In 1863 he did not make it much farther than this point. He vividly recalled how bullets from two different Union rifles hit him almost simultaneously, and he was forced to turn back. He remembered his retreat being as perilous as the advance, with swarms of bullets and shells flying past him.[12]

Also close to the road, Waldron recalled, "I saw Gen. Garnett killed. He was shot from his horse, the horse dreadfully mutilated by the shell." Whatever became of the general's body would remain unknown to Waldron and everyone else. Lost in the aftermath, the corpse went unidentified and was likely interned in a mass grave.[13] The worst for Waldron, and for many others, was yet to come. "I cannot describe," he admitted, "the terrible fire we received at the stone wall and all the way over. It was all a mistake, a terrible mistake. We all knew it but went in because we were ordered in." Waldron's memory of helplessness stemmed from what happened next. While climbing the stones, his lieutenant, Thomas Holland, went down with a wound to the neck and was taken prisoner. Calvin Dearing went across the wall with Waldron that day. He would make it no farther. Dearing went down quickly, as did his colonel, Robert Allen, victim of a musket ball to the skull. The colonel was lucid for a few more moments, Dearing remembered, before asking where the regimental flag had gone. As his commander slipped away, Dearing recalled the bizarre experience of sitting next to him and feeling almost invisible. "We lay there side by side while they fought over us and around us."[14]

Among those still locked in the struggle were Moses Waldron, John Waldron, and Thomas McDaniel. For Moses, the close-quarters fighting persisted in his memory from that very moment onward, punctuated now and then by the vision of his uncle attempting to save him and going down from an assumed lethal rifle shot. Moses apparently never learned that his uncle had actually survived the engagement. In fact, John was captured and taken to a Federal field hospital, where doctors removed a shattered left arm. Moses likely remained unaware of his uncle's survival, because the man lasted only a few more weeks, eventually dying from his injuries.[15] Moses was almost certainly one of the last from Company D to see his friend Thomas McDaniel alive. During the melee, McDaniel tried to spike one of Cushing's guns when Waldron saw him collapse from multiple gunshot wounds. Officially McDaniel was listed as missing in action. By the end of 1863 his regiment presumed he had been killed. Likely,

PICKETT'S MEN AT BLOODY ANGLE

Veterans of Pickett's Division were told to halt some twenty paces away from
the Angle and listen to more orations. Their greater desire was to speak
with fellow survivors located on the other side of the wall. (Courtesy George
Grantham Bain Collection, Library of Congress)

Thomas was deposited in the same set of mass graves in which Garnett
had been buried. Overall, the day's casualty rate for Garnett's Brigade was
65 percent. Moses's 28th Virginia lost 28 killed, 86 wounded, and 106
captured, or nearly 90 percent of their original number.[16]

At the Reunion, as similar memories swirled in the minds of the survivors, the organizers instructed the gray line to halt and fan out some
thirty paces away from their countrymen standing on the other side of
the vine-covered wall. At this critical moment, with the veterans facing
each other, the Gettysburg Commission deemed it appropriate and fitting to treat the men to another speech.

Given the honor was forty-nine-year-old US Rep. J. Hampton Moore
of Pennsylvania's Third District, an electorate that included Philadelphia. As such, Moore ostensibly acted as the Philadelphia Brigade's political spokesperson. Stepping upon the iconic wall, he stood on the rocks
and gave a blow-by-blow account of Pickett's Charge. In a prolonged oration, Moore used the word "you" no fewer than forty times, describing
what the veterans supposedly did, and often assuming what they were
thinking during the fight. To the listeners, this may have been a considerable reach for the congressman, seeing that he was born a year after

Veterans and civilians crowd the Angle moments before US Representative Moore delivers a lengthy speech. Visible to the upper left is the monument to the 72nd Pennsylvania. The flag of the Union Army 2nd Corps, 2nd Division, is visible to the upper right. (Courtesy George Grantham Bain Collection, Library of Congress)

the battle, had no military experience himself, and his professional training consisted almost entirely of bank management. Throughout, Moore depicted this peaceful reenactment not as a dynamic combination of personal searches and small reunions but as a singular declaration of allegiance to the nation-state, in his words, "mindful of your past differences only as thrilling reminiscences in the story of your lives, you are manifesting the highest, the truest, forms of patriotism."[17]

Moore then proceeded to speak of the violent engagement in strangely wistful terms: "With shot for shot and bayonet for bayonet you met each other then; now, when the musket and the saber rest amongst the treasured trophies of war, you look into each other's eyes, you swap again your countless tales of perilous adventure, knowing, each of you, on either side, what all the world concedes, that those with whom you contended were 'foemen worthy of your steel.'"[18]

The congressman's graphic wording evidently did not appeal to the audience. Journalists described the speech as simply "long." Moore con-

Rep. J. Hampton Moore at the Angle, advancing the mythos of fearlessness in Pickett's Charge and proclaiming close-quarter combat as the embodiment of patriotism. (Courtesy George Grantham Bain Collection, Library of Congress)

tinued to pepper survivors with phrases like "those who clubbed their guns and turned you back," "the impact of heavy guns; the mad trample of the wounded chargers," and "the most terrific hand-to-hand encounter of the war."[19] Well-intended as it may have been, Moore's address was not the first time that organizers ran interference. In February 1913, members of Pickett's Division and the Philadelphia Brigade Association petitioned the Gettysburg Commission to allow them to camp side by side at the Reunion. Officials denied the request, explaining that such an undertaking would be "difficult."[20]

When Moore finally ended his step-by-step recounting, he paused, and continued, "Since the days of Betsy Ross . . . " As one reporter noted, he "spoke at some length of the valor of both sides and the sublimity of the reunion, while the merciless sun fairly roasted his audience and caused one old man to be borne away on a stretcher." Moore eventually moved on to a theme of US supremacy on the world stage, extolling the virtues of national expansion through the war with Mexico and the conquest of imperial Spain in Cuba and the Philippines. Finally, he ended with an assurance to his aged audience, "You . . . may now return to your homes to await the last muster, conscious when the final summons comes that you can face eternity with the mantle of charity and kindness covering the last vestige of enmity that may have found a lurking place in your hearts."[21]

Informed yet again that they were all about to die soon, the veterans had to wait still longer as the opposing flag bearers crossed their standards above the wall, with a third holding the Stars and Stripes aloft above them. After a brief pause, the veterans were finally allowed to engage each other, and the crowd of thousands roared its approval.[22] What followed closely resembled what had been going on since their trains first rolled into town. Some simply reached across the stones to shake hands. Several helped each other over the wall. Some embraced. Most slowly climbed over the rocks to explore the landscape and talk to one another. A few began to weep while others laughed. Nearly all were tired. They had been standing at the wall for nearly half an hour.[23]

During the speech, William Marston of the 56th Virginia was shocked to see a familiar face among the Philadelphians. He approached the person afterward and said, "You are the man I shot behind the field gun just [as] you turned us back." After some hesitation, the man to whom he was speaking, Arthur Applegate of the 72nd Pennsylvania, responded, "No, it was my brother Fred. I remember you had a rag with blood on it around your head, and you shot with—"

"A pistol," returned Marston.

Applegate then extended his hand to Marston, trying to find an appropriate response to a man who had just confessed to shooting his brother. Applegate uttered, "Maybe I shot your brother, if you lost one."[24]

By this time, onlookers, journalists, and veterans had intertwined. Visitors and family took photographs and shook veterans' hands while the soldiers themselves became engrossed in shared stories. Repeatedly, they sought connections. "Are you Pickett, too?" or "You from Pittsburgh?"[25]

A common practice was to try to piece together a clearer picture of what eluded them on their own, to try to make sense of one of the most chaotic and traumatic episodes of their lives. When a group of Virginians asked C. E. Scouten of the 59th New York if he saw any of Pickett's men make it over the wall, he said he only saw Armistead. "I saw no one else. Still, you must remember that it wasn't possible to keep tabs on everything that was going on just then." One former Federal marveled how much of the landscape had changed, yet it was familiar enough to unearth a lingering guilt. "There was a deep depression just over there where I am pointing, and a lot of you got huddled in there, and my company just poured shot into you and slaughtered you like flies. But the hole isn't there now. It has been filled in over the years. Everything is different."[26]

Though organized in regiments, divisions, and states, the survivors repeatedly showed a preference for small, intimate groups as a means of addressing memory. Columnist George Fleming approached Moses Waldron and his little circle standing near the wall. When asked what he remembered of the assault, Waldron offered dissonance to Congressman Moore's heroic version: "We did not march back in good order. It was every man for himself."[27]

Watching them connect with each other, Fleming wrote, "I looked at these quiet, gentle, old men and it was hard to believe that they were survivors of Pickett's men, representative of the finest type of the American

Popularly seen as the Reunion's pinnacle event, the staged moment (*above*) actually received marginal attention when it transpired. John Heiser, historian at Gettysburg National Military Park, finds that this "Hands across the Wall" photo was taken soon after the Pickett's Charge ceremony concluded, when veterans were milling about and the photographer and officials gathered these fellows together. (*Fiftieth Anniversary of the Battle of Gettysburg: Report of the Pennsylvania Commission*)

soldier." The opportunity to talk about their experiences with fellow survivors drove several men to tears. Veteran George Stackhouse confessed,
"There wasn't a dry eye among us. It seemed to me I could hear the roar
of artillery and the crackle of musketry all over again. Then I thought of
the years that had passed and, as I gripped the hand of a man in gray, I
thought of how it was our last meeting on earth." A Louisville reporter
added, "No American worthy the name could have witnessed that meeting and that ceremony today without experiencing a full-grown desire to
cry like a baby."[28]

Though his regiment fought near the Angle, Heman Allen declined to
attend. Allen may have begged off because he didn't want to remember, at
least within the confines of the staged proceedings. As a company clerk,
he spent much of his war alongside commanding officers, and among
them he felt closest to his first lieutenant, John Sinnot. During Pickett's
assault, the 13th Vermont stood south-southwest of the wall, scything
down Pickett's Charge from its right flank. Allen and Sinnot were near
each other when the Confederate artillery unleashed. Allen vividly recalled what happened next: "We were lying behind the slight protection
of rails, etc., which we had gathered together and had been in that un-
comfortable position for some time; the men were uneasy, some of them
would stand up to gaze over the rails to see what the conditions were in
front, [Sinnot] raised up to caution the men, saying, 'Boys, lie down or
you'll surely be hit.'"

Almost immediately after the lieutenant warned his men, a piece of
flying shrapnel smashed into his forehead, mortally wounding him. The
sight and sound of the impact remained with Allen ever since. Sinnot's
body was later buried in the Vermont section of the newly formed Gettysburg National Cemetery. Whether Allen went to see the gravesite during the Reunion, he did not say, but he could not bring himself to relive
the anniversary.[29]

For most of the postwar era, Allen chose monuments as his coping
method, erecting stone and metal memorials across the Northeast. He did
the same at the Jubilee, dedicating a monument far away from the Angle,
for a man with whom he had no direct connection. Around 3 P.M., when
Waldron was taking his first choreographed steps to the Angle, Allen was
making his way to the western base of Big Round Top, just south of Devil's
Den. It was there that Allen and associates would unveil the First Vermont

Lt. John Sinnot, a year before his death at Gettysburg. (*Pictorial History, Thirteenth Vermont Regiment*)

Heman Allen as he appeared in 1862. (*Pictorial History, Thirteenth Vermont Regiment*)

Cavalry Monument, near to the hour when that force slammed against the extreme Confederate right.

Altogether, this one ceremony had twenty-nine speakers on the docket, including two ex-governors; sitting Vermont governor Allen Fletcher; a US senator; a number of Vermont veterans from across the country; the last surviving Confederate major general, Evander Law; and the unreconstructed Felix Robertson (who proceeded to tell the audience that Jefferson Davis was the "greatest statesman of our time"). Allen was tenth in line, just after a brief overview from *National Tribune* editor John McElroy on "the American soldier of 1861–1866" and two orators teaming up to speak on "The Old Vermont Brigade," leading one to wonder if the entire dedication ceremony would last until the weekend.[30]

When Allen finally rose, he was brief and plain in speech. He simply mentioned the work of the cavalry regiment's first chaplain, John Woodward. Allen added that a memorial had been erected the previous year in Woodward's hometown of Westford, recognizing all the young men from that place who had left for the war, although that homage featured only the likeness of Chaplain Woodward. The same would be for this new monument. Technically venerating the entire regiment, the shrine would become known as the Wells Monument, because it featured a grandiose statue of the unit's commander, Maj. Gen. William Wells.[31]

This was actually the regiment's second monument at Gettysburg. The first, dedicated in 1889 and positioned a few hundred paces northeast, looked markedly different. It resembled most cenotaphs of the 1870s and 1880s. Stout, low to the ground, and understated, the monolith emphasized presence, labor, and loss. The central message was a solemn tally of the unit's casualties. Among the words carved into its side, the First Vermont Cavalry Monument read: "Took part in the battles of Gettysburg, Wilderness, Yellow Tavern, Winchester, Cedar Creek, Waynesboro, Five Forks, Appomattox Station and 67 other battles and engagements. Aggregate 2297 officers and men. Killed and mortally wounded in action 102; died of disease and by accidents 123; died in Confederate prisons 172—total 397. Total wounded in action 275."

In contrast, the Wells Monument of 1913 was erected predominantly by and for later generations. These structures were consistently taller, far more ornate, even celebratory, emphasizing valor and orders of battle. They also conveyed the message of human sacrifice for national salvation. In the Wells Monument's own words: "The 1st Battalion and part of the 3rd Lt. Col. A. W. Preston commanding were ordered to the lane and struck Law's Brigade in the flank. The onset was terrific, sabres and bayonets, revolvers and muskets being freely used. After a struggle the hill was carried by the 1st Vermont. . . . This memorial signalizes the valor of the officers and the men of the First Vermont Cavalry who here paid to the nation the uttermost tribute of devotion."

Although a dying notion in the discipline of history, the "Great Man Theory" enjoyed a resurgence among the masses who desired a simpler, more heroic version of the past. This trend, to which social and political leaders were often partial, also reflected a marginalization of the common person. Advocating the superhuman-as-prime-mover view were those who commissioned the Wells memorial, including Adj. Gen. of Vermont Theodore S. Peck. Though Peck had briefly served as a private in the 1st Vermont Cavalry, he was not with that regiment at the time of Gettysburg. He was nonetheless invited to speak at the dedication, to describe both the monument he sanctioned and the charge he never saw. Of the latter, Peck said, "No more gallant or more desperate charge was made during

The Wells Monument dedication, where many of the spoken tributes were as hyperbolic as the monument itself. (*Fiftieth Anniversary of the Battle of Gettysburg: Report of the Pennsylvania Commission*)

the war, nor one more fruitless. This was but a single holocaust—one of many offered on the altar of American Freedom." *Holocaust* is an ancient Greek word meaning "sacrificial burnt offering."[32]

Gettysburg's shift from solemn memorials to triumphant monuments mimicked what was occurring in town squares and city parks across the country. The most conspicuous manifestation transpired mere months before the Reunion. For years, Congress debated how to federally memorialize Abraham Lincoln on the centennial of his birth. Lawmakers eventually reduced a multitude of suggestions down to two options: a highway running from Washington, DC, to Gettysburg or an adulatory monument within the capital itself.

By February 1913 the monument campaigners prevailed, although critics remained vocal. Rep. William Borland of Missouri mocked the project as "the little Greek temple down by the brewery" and predicted future generations would care for it even less. In response, Joseph Gurney Cannon of Illinois chastised such thinking as unpatriotic, believing that hero worship through monuments was a public virtue. He also had specific heroes in mind, proclaiming, "Washington, Lincoln, Lee, and Jefferson Davis were the greatest men in American history."[33]

A great many agreed. Inspired by the triumphant rhetoric of "reconciliation," Southern nationalists called for CSA idols of granite and marble to be built in the North. Emboldened by the mutual admiration speeches pouring from the Gettysburg Reunion, Daniel Smith Gordon of the Washington, DC, Columbia Historical Society wrote an open letter to the *Baltimore Sun* insisting that the government erect a statue of Robert E. Lee in the nation's capital. The *Houston Post* proclaimed, "With that Gettysburg reunion in full blast, nothing remains of the old quarrel save Whittier's poems and the absence of a system of Confederate monuments in New England. We must now proceed to burn the poems and erect the monuments."[34]

Much like crusades and other military campaigns, monuments were attempts to project ownership of place; hence the proliferation of Confederate monuments in Southern parks and squares during the era of Jim Crow, and the planting of Federal monuments and national cemeteries across the Southern landscape in the years and decades following the Civil War.

If more closely inspected, the tablature and architecture surrounding the Peace Jubilee would have well exemplified this ongoing battle over public space, not only between North and South but also between states and regiments. A flood of construction during the battle's twenty-fifth anniversary produced a strange contest of hubris, with regiments arguing over who advanced farthest, and few agreeing on where officers fell or flanks stood. In an adroit move, the Gettysburg Battlefield Memorial Association established a "Line of Battle" rule, requiring monuments to be placed only where units entered the fight, which left Confederate markers far away from prestigious locations such as Cemetery Ridge, Cemetery Hill, and Little Round Top. Although depicted as "history," the subsequent ornamentations reflected the unsettled postwar atmosphere.[35]

Regardless of their political origins, memorials did have a practical use at the Reunion. Veterans used specific shrines as invaluable points of contact. Tented as they were by states in which they currently resided, many survivors like Fickas and Waldron struggled to find their scattered companies. Through formal and informal gatherings, tributes served as landmarks around which the lost could be found. Minnesotans gathered around the Cemetery Ridge Monument to their 1st Infantry Regiment all week long and heard their governor deliver a heartfelt speech to their dead on the morning of July 3 (a day after the anniversary of that regiment's costly defense of Cemetery Ridge). Around the plaza of Pennsylvania's sprawling dedication, survivors from the Keystone State collected in front of their respective bronze tablets, each listing every member of every battery and regiment present at the battle. For Fickas's US Artillery Battery G, there was the granite and bronze cenotaph on Blocher's Knoll and a second in the National Cemetery between the towering New York State Monument and the Soldiers' Monument. The homage to Allen's 13th Vermont was quite familiar to him; he was present at its dedication in 1899. Positioned south of the Copse of Trees and the Great Tent, near where the unit stood on July 3, the structure embodied a narrative in transition. Its granite base and bronze tablets offer somber depictions of the regiment's movements and losses, while a seven-foot statue of Lt. Stephen F. Brown, with captured Confederate sword in hand, offered yet another example of the immortal savior figure.[36]

For Hodges and Waldron, their memorials consisted of a modest tablet each, simply depicting the work of their larger brigades. Both markers stood upon Seminary Ridge along West Confederate Avenue. In the words of a Union veteran who gazed upon them, "These markers are all alike and consist of a round pedestal of dark polished granite, about three feet in diameter and six or seven feet high, with a bronze tablet about four or five feet in size resting on the top at an angle of about 45 degrees and suitably inscribed." The sign for Brig. Gen. Robert Hoke's brigade, to which Hodges's 21st North Carolina belonged, stood close to his tent and may have served as a rallying point for his comrades.[37]

For the more patriotic, with whom Hodges, Fickas, and Waldron did not associate much, these understated tablets failed to inspire. Among the disappointed, Col. Archibald Boyden chastised his fellow North Carolinians: "It's a shame upon the state that she has let 50 years pass and no monument here to mark the great deeds of her men. I trust this great reunion will bring about the patriotism and that immediately a monument fund will be started to erect not merely a shaft, but a temple of fame so that the great historians may be able to get their bearings on what North Carolina did."[38]

Historians were already aware of what the Tar Heels had done at Gettysburg. The state sent nearly forty regiments and batteries, and it lost more troops in the contest than Virginia: sixty-seven hundred killed, wounded, captured, or missing compared to forty-nine hundred. But in Boyden's eye, style outweighed substance.[39]

Needling the likes of Boyden further, the base for the enormous Virginia State Monument was already complete. Upon the memorial's completion in 1917, the veritable bastion exemplified Great Man Theory in excess. Covering nearly a thousand square feet, at its center stood a team of seven figures, young and old, representing the citizen-soldiers of Old Virginia. Dressed in homespun cloth, standing over the debris of combat, they guarded a mighty pedestal twenty-four feet high. Upon that grand pillar towered Robert E. Lee, mounted on his beloved steed Traveller. In direct contrast with the haggard mortals at his feet, Lee appeared pristine, composed, literally larger than life, and primed for reverence.[40]

Hodges's North Carolina would have its monument, but not until 1929. By then the horrors of the Great War in Europe dampened the nation's desire for martial ostentation. The result was a subdued, reflective memorial to the suffering: three lifelike soldiers facing an uncertain destiny, and a wounded comrade urging them forward. Adding to the human element, the faces were modeled after actual veterans.[41]

Regardless of the public contests, veterans at the Reunion continued to seek private conversations. Walking about the battlefield park among the tents and avenues, a New Yorker observed, "As a soldier of the Union army would point out a monument erected to his regiment or brigade, they would sit about on the green grass, Union and Confederate, and discuss the points of the great battle."[42]

As dusk crept over the fields on July 3, and the lamps and campfires began to speckle the camp with gilded points of light, the talking cures would continue to ebb and flow. But something was coming that would break the rhythm and stir the darkest of memories. At nightfall, organizers unveiled one more event. As a tribute to the men, there would be an enormous, elongated fireworks display. The undertaking was so large that construction required teams of engineers, electricians, and carpenters. Miners were brought in to alter the hillsides of Little Round Top. Per the *Philadelphia Inquirer*, "To set several of the larger pieces, it was necessary to blast resting places in the side of the mountain." All would be worth it, claimed the Pennsylvania Commission, promising the show would be second to none.[43]

The spectacle was originally scheduled for July 4, but a succession of late announcements from Washington—former President Taft and Chief Justice White declining to attend, President Wilson's initial indications that he would also not appear, Congress eventually refusing to fund the highly anticipated Peace Memorial—led planners to move the event to the night of July 3. The sheer enormity of pyrotechnics, ten train cars' worth, drew tourists by the tens of thousands from Baltimore, Philadelphia, Washington, and beyond. An estimated fourteen thousand automobiles circled the park, and according to the Anniversary Commission, their headlights produced "a scene that seemed as though thousands of gigantic fireflies were silently, swiftly, moving through the darkness of the night, throughout the great battlefield's length and breadth." A reporter on the ground offered a different perspective, noting that the swarming traffic posed a danger for the roaming veterans.[44]

At 8:45 P.M., near the summit of Little Round Top, a bright flash erupted from the mouth of a three-inch ordnance cannon, signaling the tempest's unleashing. As its report rolled across the encampment, a storm of din and color showered the valley below. With poetic license, columnist O. H. Stewart told his *Washington Herald* readers: "The dawn of a new era was sounded, a solid reunited America. . . . Following the firing of this gun there was the most elaborate display of fireworks perhaps ever seen anywhere, witnessed not only by the united armies of the North and the South, nearly 60,000 strong, but by thousands and thousands of their relatives and friends from all over the country and by practically all of Gettysburg and the surrounding country."[45]

Stewart's depiction was very much like the commemoration altogether. The verbiage from above did not always reflect realities on the ground. The great host of sixty thousand veterans was by the evening of July 3 more along the lines of thirty thousand. Even as night descended, thousands were embarking on trains and in automobiles to return to their points of origin. For those still in camp, some enjoyed the show, but as one reporter confessed, "Even this display was unable to hold the veterans." Greater effort was placed on visiting friends old and new, taking in the sites in town, or resting after another long day in the heat.[46]

The show's finale was supposed to be a giant 120-foot by 200-foot pyrotechnic American flag near the crest of Little Round Top, set aflame in sparks of red, white, and blue. When the bright tribute became enveloped and obscured by its own spewing smoke, spectators were left wondering if something had gone wrong.[47]

For others, the presentation resonated too closely to the sights, sounds, and smells of combat. As one observer wrote, the choreography included "a great salvo of dynamite guns and belching mortars." Another described how "hundreds of batteries of rockets, roman candles, and other fireworks . . . were exploded, hurling long sizzling serpents into the air and sending colored shooters far out over the battlefield and the tents of the veterans encamped there." Although the term did not yet exist, post-traumatic stress disorder did afflict a large proportion of the war's survivors, and relapses were possible well into later life. Common triggers included loud noises and bright flashes of light, which would have been difficult to avoid in the encampment. The Pennsylvania Commission estimated the explosions went on for nearly two hours.[48]

The intense barrage's commendable aspect, reasoned the *Pittsburgh Daily Post*, was that at least it did not transpire on July 4. There was something to be said for a subdued Independence Day. The paper was certainly not the first to recommend solemnity. By the turn of the century, advances in mass production and chemical industries made pyrotechnics relatively cheap and widely available to the general public, who proceeded to blow things up, including themselves, in an annual burst of patriotic fervor. To quell the carnage, a growing number of parents, magistrates, and medical workers endorsed a "safe and sane" approach to the holiday, with measurable success. From 1900 to 1913, the number of fires, injuries, and deaths had fallen considerably. Read in situ, the *Post* article could also be interpreted as a challenge to the hawkish language delivered time and again at Gettysburg. The paper had reporters on-site, who may have taken issue with the death and glory narrative, especially when juxtaposed with the innumerable scenes of veterans seeking amity:

> The public welcomes relief from the noisy and dangerous celebration of this great anniversary. There is a growing disposition to get away from the methods that kill and maim. The casualties of the last half century total into the thousands. . . . This justifies the "safe and sane" movement. The anniversary is the one day of the year that Americans should celebrate, but not in a manner to make it as bloody as a battle and to burn up millions in property as a result of recklessness and folly. . . . People can make the most of it without the horror of a list of dead and injured.[49]

CHAPTER 8

"National Day"

> "So Christ was once offered to bear the sins of many; and unto them that look for him shall he appear the second time without sin unto salvation."
> —*HEBREWS*, 9:28

The second coming did not proceed exactly as planned. The chosen were less inclined to hear sermons than to find their own way. This dissonance was never more pronounced than on the Fourth of July. Before the Great Reunion officially began, the *Pittsburgh Press* predicted the nation's birthday would "culminate in a patriotic rally eclipsing anything ever before arranged in this country." Nothing of the sort happened. The *Press*'s rival, the *Pittsburgh Daily Post*, found instead, "many of the Pittsburghers attended the reunions in the big tent this morning, although more of them preferred to wander through the shady lanes in the National Cemetery."[1] By far, the glorious Fourth would prove to be the most subdued of all days and officially end with a discreet ceremony.

In its final official report, the Gettysburg Anniversary Commission explained why the highly anticipated climax failed to materialize:

Friday morning, July 4th, no reunions in the Great Tent had been scheduled, as it was originally this Commission's desire to there hold Peace Jubilee services, starting at 10:00 o'clock that morning, with the Chief Justice of the United States Supreme Court presiding, and the President of the United States to deliver the oration, and, at high noon, dedicate the site for

Boy Scouts load yet another heat victim into an awaiting ambulance. Aid stations and hospitals received nearly ten thousand walk-ins and emergencies, ranging from stomach ailments to heart failure. The most common cases involved heat exhaustion, which killed at least two attendees, required hospitalization for over three hundred, and affected several thousand. (Courtesy George Grantham Bain Collection, Library of Congress)

a Great Peace Memorial. But it appearing during the closing hours of the summer session of the late Congress (62nd), that no action could be had at its hands to make such a Peace Memorial possible, and both the President and the Chief Justice having declined the invitations of this Commission to be present as its Guests of Honor, and to participate in the Great Reunion, all these services on July 4th had to be abandoned, the fireworks of the evening before having been arranged as the closing event of the Reunion.[2]

The camp itself gave clear signs of winding down. Departed trains filled to capacity. Quartermaster wagon teams rolled up and down the tent-lined streets gathering blankets and lanterns. Among items lost and found were seventeen sets of false teeth, a multitude of jackets and keys, stacks of crutches, an artificial leg, and a revolver. At breakfast, kitchen staff piled surplus food onto the mess plates. Field hospital directors began sending their remaining patients to the state hospital in Harrisburg. F. E. Ruslander of the *Pittsburgh Daily Post* hit close to the mark when he led his daily report with the headline, "Home Thoughts Uppermost in Veterans' Minds."[3]

When Woodrow Wilson belatedly reversed his decision on June 28, organizers reinserted him into the sparse July 4 schedule. Political prudence rather than personal desire influenced Wilson to finally accept the invitation. With newspapers present from all four corners of the country, and the event proving to be a national success story, this was an opportunity to solidify his image. Just eight months earlier, Woodrow Wilson's own succession to the White House came about from a fragmented electorate. Garnering less than 42 percent of the popular vote, he likely would have lost had the Republicans not split between progressives and conservatives. The election also brought several Socialists to local positions, and over 6 percent of voters sided with the party's presidential candidate Eugene Debs. As the first Southern-born president elected since the Civil War, chairing a country bitterly fractured over how it should proceed into the future, Wilson felt obligated to play the unifier role. He cabled his wife Ellen on June 28, explaining why he had to spend the holiday away from her: "Find so long as I am President, I can be nothing else." Most chief executives since Lincoln had visited Gettysburg, but this would be only the second time that a sitting president would deliver a formal oration on the battlefield.[4]

Wilson's train arrived from Baltimore a few moments before 11 A.M., and as the president disembarked, a twenty-one-gun salute from the Third US Artillery pounded the morning air. Accompanied by Pennsylvania's governor Tener, Wilson stepped into a convertible for the mile-plus trek to the Great Tent. Escorting him were battalions from the Fifth US Cavalry and Fifth US Infantry, in yet another attempt to make the proceedings more military than civilian. Down the Emmitsburg Pike the caravan motored, with the Pennsylvania constabulary cordoning off the sides of the road. For many veterans, this would be the only glimpse they would get of their head of state. Lincoln spent twenty-four hours during his visit. Wilson would stay less than forty-five minutes.[5]

The Wilson-Tener motorcade parked near the tent's main entrance. Surrounded by well-wishers and gawkers, the party made for the opening.

President Wilson addresses a near-capacity crowd in the Great Tent. The collateral din of the crowd inside and automobile traffic outside made much of his speech barely audible. (Courtesy George Grantham Bain Collection, Library of Congress)

At the insistence of press photographers, Wilson paused for a moment to have his picture taken between two veterans, each dressed in their opposing uniforms. He then entered to a raucous cheer of a near-capacity crowd, and the band at the center of the tent began to play "Hail to the Chief." No more than half of the ten thousand present were veterans. Said a reporter, "Most people regarded the ceremonies as more of a civic celebration, more of the usual Fourth of July affair, than as a large episode of the reunion."[6]

Dressed in a black frock coat, with his speech in his left hand, Wilson stepped to the front of the stage after a brief introduction from Tener and proceeded to offer his own Gettysburg Address. It sounded strangely like a diluted version of Lincoln's original: "But do we deem the Nation completed and finished? These venerable men crowding here to this famous field have set us a great example of devotion and utter sacrifice. They were willing to die that the people might live. But their task is done. Their day is turned into evening. They look to us to perfect what they established."⁷

Similar though they were, Wilson's message contained pointed differences to Lincoln's. Lincoln did not directly condemn the Confederate experiment, yet neither did he praise the Confederate soldier. The men of whom he spoke were exclusively Union. Further, he interpreted the Federal deceased as "those who here gave their lives that that nation might live."

In contrast, much like the overriding official narrative of the Jubilee, Wilson's message heralded both warring parties, and was overtly messianic. "They [Confederate and Union] were willing to die that the people might live. . . . We are made by these tragic, epic things to know what it costs to make a nation—the blood and sacrifice of multitudes of unknown men lifted to a great stature in the view of all generations by knowing no limit to their manly willingness to serve." Though Lincoln came to commemorate a burial site, he chose to focus on the living. Wilson arrived upon an amalgamation of the living and spoke mostly of the dead. Foremost, he painted warfare in nationalistic terms, using superlatives such as "gallant," "glory," "heroic days of war," "patriotic fervor," and "valor," words that Lincoln did not include. Most conspicuously, Lincoln's address also did not contain the term "sacrifice," yet Wilson inserted it three times.⁸ Such militaristic rhetoric might seem utterly out of character from the future architect of the Fourteen Points, with its insistence on maritime neutrality, disarmament, and a League of Nations. But his was the nation with a Monroe Doctrine and the Open Door. Though Wilson labored diligently to avoid entanglements with empires, he was not averse to leading one himself.

There were compelling reasons to believe in American exceptionalism and a manifest destiny. Since Wilson's birth in 1856, the United States had grown from thirty-one states to forty-eight. When he was a teenager, the country ranked fourth in the world in industrial output. By his inauguration, it reigned supreme, leading the world in coal, copper, and pig iron production. Nearly two-thirds of the planet's cotton and petroleum came from the United States. The nation's steel output alone increased fifteen-hundred-fold in his lifetime, and yearly totals nearly matched the rest of the world combined. Invigorated by the recent innovation of the assembly line, automobile manufacturing easily outpaced that of all other nations. Annually the country grew enough corn to give every person on Earth an entire bushel and still have nearly a half-billion more bushels left over.[9]

Arguably, his was a United States of the Americas and the Pacific, where in his lifetime the nation either bought or conquered Alaska, Guam, Hawaii, the Philippines, Puerto Rico, and Wake. The long-awaited Panama Canal would be operational in a year. When Wilson was delivering his speech, Gen. John Pershing was leading an assault upon indigenous peoples on the island of Jolo in the Philippines, while other US forces occupied portions of Cuba, Mexico, and Nicaragua. Wilson was sincere when he told his listeners, "Here is a great people, great with every force that has ever beaten in the lifeblood of mankind. And it is secure. There is no one within its borders, there is no power among the nations of the earth to make it afraid."[10]

Several journalists praised the speech, and a lot of papers printed it in full, but many veterans expressed disappointment. Background noise in and outside the tent muffled Wilson's words. Old Federals were vexed that he never mentioned Lincoln. An Indiana reporter noticed that Wilson was only interrupted "once or twice with cheering," while another stated, "President Wilson failed to stir the heart of the veterans. . . . Not once was he interrupted by a handclap or a cheer."[11] A Capt. John C. Delaney said, "Even the forced remarks of President Wilson were well received, but how tame beside the fewer words of our Lincoln." Vermonter A. W. Willey waited nearly two hours in a prime seat to hear his president's speech, only to find that "he read it very scholarly but there was not much enthusiasm." Pennsylvania veteran Jacob Cress was even less kind, calling the address "a very poor thing for a president of this great republic."[12]

In fairness, possibly any oration Wilson could have delivered would have paled in comparison to Lincoln's exalted address. But what deflated his presentation most involved what he did next. Immediately after finishing, Wilson exited the rear of the tent and climbed into a waiting car. With no inspection of the camp, no further interaction with veterans or the general public, he motored away to begin his summer vacation. Had the commander in chief remained a few minutes longer, he would have shared in one of the most transcendent moments of the entire anniversary.[13]

As the president and entourage motored away, the church bells in town chimed the noon hour. On schedule, a lone bugle sounded over the

President Wilson exiting the Great Tent after his address. Within minutes, he was out of Gettysburg. (Courtesy George Grantham Bain Collection, Library of Congress)

encampment, and all US flags at each organizational headquarters were lowered to half-staff. For five straight minutes thereafter, every veteran who was capable stood at attention in remembrance of those who had died before him. The only break in silence consisted of forty-eight intermittent cannon salutes from the Third US Artillery, representing all the states then in the Union. "There was an eloquence in the silent tribute," said one participant, "that by comparison made all the Gettysburg speechmaking seem rather cheap and tawdry."[14]

Considering the moment's solemnity, one wonders if H. H. Hodges could bring himself to picture the many neighbors he lost, or the men he watched die from his Richmond hospital bed at war's end. Did Moses Waldron think of the men in his company who only lived to their teens or early twenties? What did William Fickas see in his mind during those five long minutes, every time the artillery sounded? Did he envision the scores of men his battery leveled, or the countless horses dismembered by returning fire? Could Heman Allen bring himself to recall the voice of his lieutenant and friend, John Sinnot, before Lee's artillery silenced the young officer, or the names he registered as casualties in his role as company clerk, or the increasing number of friends and acquaintances he helped bury as time claimed them one by one?

When the staccato blast of cannon ceased, and the flags returned to their apogees, the camp slowly stirred again. There was the last meal to eat and good-byes to offer. Thousands flocked to the depot and waited in the sun. Looking back at what had transpired, James Farrell of Pittsburgh surmised, "Enough tears have been shed on the historic spot during the last week to fill a large and salty pond." He watched as the attendees made final efforts to see sites of meaning and heard men say the same utterances he heard all week: "This is the spot where I lost my arm," or, "My best friend fell here." Farrell wondered what questions remained for them, but he believed that nearly all were confident about one thing. Gettysburg was a place "few if any of them ever expect to see again."[15]

As night fell, so did the population of the tent city. Walking about in search of a story, Farrell came upon a large group of veterans circled around a boisterous camp kitchen, the tent alive with shouts and laughter. Peering through the bystanders, he viewed a group of African American cooks, relaxing after a long week's exhausting work. Farrell then saw how they were making light of the moment. In the center of the tent, the kitchen staff members were reenacting a human auction: "One huge negro was placed on a stand. Another one acted as barker, shouting at the top of his voice, calling upon the assembly to bid on this person he had for sale. 'He's a fine big fellow, 5 feet 10 inches tall, sound of wind and limbs, weighing 175 pounds. Any gent in the crowd can have him for $100. Come, what will you bid?'"

Workmates laughed at the spectacle. Farrell noticed that the first impulse among the older onlookers was to laugh along. The collective noise attracted more people. In a short while, however, the jocularity turned uneasy. It was then, he noted, "it could be seen that they were affected by the unusual and startling recollection of a state of affairs which had helped materially precipitate the awful war they are survivors of." The entire scene, Farrell observed, felt "almost gruesome."[16]

EPILOGUE

To the Dying Departed

"All day weary veterans walked over the dusty roads and streets to the rail-road stations . . . and stood or sat around, many weeping under the rays of a scorching sun while the trains to take them home were being prepared. There were no flying banners, blaring bands or marching columns. The veterans came to the stations and waited patiently for the announcer with his big megaphone to tell them that their trains were made up."
—*ASSOCIATED PRESS*, July 5, 1913

On Saturday, nearly all remaining veterans packed their bags, left their tents, and started for home. In their possession was an assortment of sou-venirs. Rather than instruments of death, many of their keepsakes were living or once alive. One man saved a pine sapling, carrying it away in a small pot. Another had a branch from a tree that had shielded him in the battle. J. C. McMasters took wheat from the fields back to his Indi-ana home. A surgeon from New Orleans pocketed some oak leaves from the Copse of Trees. Many leaned on walking sticks harvested from the groves. S. H. Brown from Houston cut a long hickory branch from the area of Pickett's Charge. "My battery was attached to [Pickett's Division]," he said, "and this stick will always call to mind memories of Gettysburg."[1]

All were invited to keep their tin and acrylic mess kits, and thousands did. Others took bits of food, including souvenir hardtack made by a cracker company. Earlier a person left with two suitcases full of soil from where he fought on the second day. He was quoted as saying, "I shall make a garden box of it." One account has H. H. Hodges doing the same, taking earth from near the Angle and filling an entire case with it, then walking the mile from camp to the Western Maryland platform. He reportedly told bystanders that he wanted to take enough home to plant flowers. What is known for certain is that while waiting under a burning sun to board his train, Hodges collapsed and died.[2]

Officials worked their way through the crowd and found Hodges's body prostrate on the platform. They decided to take his remains from the depot and to a mortuary in town instead of the temporary morgue within the camp. Hours later, an examination determined the cause of death as acute cardiac dilatation (enlargement of the heart). If the diagnosis was correct, Hodges's heart stopped because of an arterial blockage or intense exertion. Regardless of what felled him, it was said that officials of the Western Maryland intended to send the soil with the deceased so that the two could be buried together.[3] He was the ninth and last reported fatality, a total that organizers believed to be commendable considering the number of elderly under their watch. Pennsylvania Health Commissioner Dr. Samuel G. Dixon credited the "low" death rate to the available medical care and "survival of the fittest." The New York *Sun* hypothesized that only nine died because "comrades were determined to live through the historic celebration." In any event, those who initially believed that the Reunion would be a dangerous undertaking for the aged later surmised that the event was actually good for their health.[4]

Yet in many instances the return trip underscored the arduous nature of the journey altogether, exemplified by the curious case of James H. Richardson, who had served in William Fickas's old regiment of the 14th Indiana. He embarked on a train bound for Indianapolis, but as it neared the destination, the only traces of Richardson were a few of his official papers found scattered in one of the compartments. His party remembered seeing him onboard for most of their trip yet had somehow lost sight of him.[5]

Days later, family members in Terre Haute and Catlin learned of his disappearance. They immediately posted his likeness in regional newspapers and begged Gov. Samuel Ralston (having recently returned from Gettysburg himself) to assist. Citizens along the route were instructed to look for an individual who was seventy-six years of age, with gray hair, 5'10", weighing 148 pounds—attributes that could apply to any number of veterans along the five-hundred-mile stretch. Richardson did possess some distinguishing features: two missing fingers, scars upon his body, and gray eyes. After four days of searching, the answer came by way of a phone call to Richardson's daughter in Catlin. Her father had perished in Ohio.[6]

During the last day of the Reunion, the heat and humidity evidently weakened Richardson as it had Hodges, to the point at which friends had to assist him onto his train. From there the searing summer sun continued to roast the passenger cars, and his rapidly dehydrating body began to shut down. When the train made a scheduled stop in Cincinnati, Richardson rose from his seat, stumbled away from his comrades without prompting their notice, and wandered into the station in what an eyewitness described as "a fit of temporary insanity." Restrained and taken to the nearby Good Samaritan Hospital, he died of heatstroke hours later. He had no documentation on his person and no one to identify him.[7]

After several days, when the body was confirmed to be Richardson, state officials in Ohio and Indiana organized the return of the remains to the waiting family. Not long after the burial services, Richardson's son and daughter received a letter of condolence from their governor, which proceeded to explain why their father had died. "It was recognized by those who undertook the trip to the great reunion," Ralston assured them, "that in the nature of things some of the old soldiers would pay for the exhausting experience with their lives. The old soldiers themselves also realized this as true. But they all felt that the good to be accomplished to the American people by such a reunion of old-time foes would more than compensate for all such sacrifices."[8]

Once again the death of an individual, in this case by exposure, was rewritten by public officials as a willing death for the nation's redemption. If Governor Ralston's assertions that "all such sacrifices" of aged men were necessary to reunify the country were valid, then apparently the balance required more than a former schoolteacher from Terre Haute or a poor farmer from rural North Carolina. On the night of July 2, John Hermance of the 67th New York was on his way home to Wellsville, New York, when he fell off the train near Canton, Pennsylvania. The following morning, railway workers found his body next to a creek. John E. Young, eighty-five, made it no farther than his niece's home in York, Pennsylvania, before passing away. On July 4, Dr. David Stewart, formerly of the Army of the Potomac, tripped and fell on his return train, breaking his hip. Taken to the Harrisburg hospital, Stewart lived until the following Wednesday. In Newark, a day after returning home, seventy-year-old William Nicholas entered a tavern, collapsed, and died. Col. C. S. Rugg perished on his way back to Tacoma, Washington. A survivor of Gettysburg and a long, emaciating imprisonment at Andersonville, the seventy-three-year-old Rugg died among his fellow veterans as their train crossed the Idaho-Washington border. A possible cause was heat exhaustion. Several others succumbed in various stages of weakness as the days passed, dying like most of the war's fatalities, not in some *Götterdämmerung* of battle but through slow and eroding illness or injury.[9]

There were also instances of intense regret. As attendees returned with stories of finding old comrades, coming to terms with difficult memories, and being cared for so splendidly, their testimonies in press and in person led several veterans who stayed behind to chastise themselves for not going. Reactions ranged from general disappointment to severe depression. A few found the dejection and guilt more than they could endure. Six days after the close of the Reunion, sitting alone in his St. Louis home, eighty-year-old John Ernst Behne decided to drink chloroform in an attempt to kill himself. Discovered and taken to the hospital, Behne was later asked why he tried to end his life. The former member of the 3rd Missouri Union regiment responded that he dreaded the thought of his fellow veterans asking him why he did not go: "I wanted to go to the reunion, and when I couldn't I became despondent. All my old comrades among the GAR in St. Louis were going and they asked me to go too, but I could not. I did not have the money and besides, I was sick. Thursday I decided to end it all. I am sorry I did it now and hope I will get well."[10]

Despite his hope, Behne died days later. He would not be alone. Philadelphian James Galloway fell into similar distress. Feeling as if he lacked the funds to join his comrades, Galloway stayed behind. He, too, drank poison. The report read, "at the close of the reunion he sank into melancholia, brooding day and night over his disappointment until he could stand it no longer and ended his life." Perhaps a similar depth of sadness befell eighty-seven-year-old James McKeever. A resident at the Soldiers Home at Kearney, New Jersey, as well as a wounded survivor of Gettysburg, McKeever simply asked his mates to bring him back a good story. They returned from the trip to find that McKeever had died in their absence on July 2.[11]

Before, during, and after, organizers and political leaders presented their creation as a purely national phenomenon. Public figures certainly had a vested, even rational, interest in selling the Reunion as proof of widespread unity. Nation-states are ethereal human constructs, the American Civil War exemplifying just how unstable they can be. In the case of the not-entirely United States in 1913, it was still a young entity wrought with adolescent anxieties. William Fickas's Arizona achieved statehood only the year before. Millions like H. H. Hodges still lived as their forebears did, in rural subsistence. Heman Allen and Moses Waldron could well remember when slavery was legal, and they lived in a country where "separate but equal" had become federal law. One in nine residents were African Americans living in varying states of segregation. Nearly one in seven residents were foreign-born, a reality that struck fear among xenophobes. Misogyny fought headlong against a long-growing female suffrage movement. In a later, successful bid for the Senate, Indiana governor Samuel Ralston received public support from a resurgent Ku Klux Klan.[12] There was also incentive to present a unified front to an increasingly agitated Europe (especially concerning the Balkans) and an emerging empire of Japan (with its recent annexation of the Korean peninsula and stunning victory in the Russo-Japanese War). More than once, the Reunion produced nationalistic threats, both veiled and direct, against the Old World and the Rising Sun.

To present an alternate universe, in which the will of the governing could be presented as the will of the governed, patriarchs had a viable unifier at their disposal, a vague but encompassing sentiment, in which a populace generally identified itself as being both American and Abrahamic. To the people, Woodrow Wilson and others presented the living and dead of Gettysburg as beatified saviors of the nation: "These venerable men crowding here to this famous field have set us a great example of devotion and utter sacrifice."[13]

Few openly questioned this soldier-as-savior narrative. The impulse among most was to accept and even advance this premise of being a chosen nation, having attained everlasting life through the martyrdom of perfect men, and to many, the Battle of Gettysburg was the Passion. The Fifth Baptist Church in Washington, DC, hosted a post-Reunion service, featuring pastor of the church J. E. Briggs (a descendant of a Confederate soldier) and local GAR commander Thomas McKee. The title of their sermon about the deadliest battle in North American history was "The Leadership of God." At a gathering of GAR members in Cambridge, Ohio, the state's governor James Cox told the audience after his return from the Jubilee: "The Almighty was the commander at Gettysburg. . . . Every blessing we enjoy today is due to these old boys." Speaking at a Fourth of July celebration in Logan, Pennsylvania, Congressman J. Washington Logue informed his audience, "Now celebrating the fiftieth anniversary of the battle of Gettysburg . . . we find a united country, glorifying the successful termination of that battle. Both North and South of our great land join in jubilation. Looking backwards, no one speaks of a lost cause."[14]

Yet even as Allen, Fickas, and Waldron returned home, as did Hodges's body, there were clear indications that the warm feelings and promotions of peace generated at Gettysburg were fleeting. About the time Hodges's remains were crossing the Mason-Dixon Line, Gov. William Hodges Mann of Virginia vehemently rejected emerging talk of Richmond hosting a 1915 jubilee: "There is absolutely no foundation for the statement that I advocated such a reunion. The friendly gathering of American citizens who were soldiers in both armies on the field of Gettysburg was a very different thing from the proposed celebration of the passing and fall of the Confederacy. I participated with pleasure and pride in the celebration this week at Gettysburg, but any reunion to commemorate the fall and burning of Richmond would be woefully inappropriate."[15]

There was also talk at the Reunion of unifying the GAR and the UCV, but the idea did not reach fruition, nor did a bill to offer federal pensions to former Confederates.[16] So moved by what he read of the week's events, US Representative Johnson of South Carolina proposed a national Civil War veterans' reunion every year. Few shared his vision.[17] Certain circles even began to downgrade the Reunion itself, including a Virginia editor who painted the event as an elaborate ruse: "Gettysburg was a fortuitous prize package coupon for the Northern and Federal section of the country. . . . Gettysburg looms very large and precious to that people. . . . Gettysburg was a Fourth of July racket—and what a great racket it was, too. But what of the forty other battles, in which McDowell, McClellan, Pope, Burnside, Hooker, and other martial geniuses that met the same army that lined up under Lee and won two battles out of three at Gettysburg? Think we're going to forget those forty other big fights and big victories? Guess not!"[18]

In Gettysburg itself, merchants noticed a surge of white visitors from the South in the weeks and months that followed. Said one man, the national coverage "has practically opened up an entirely new field of tourist trade." Pragmatically, locals quickly learned how to appeal to specific audiences, realizing that sectional loyalties were still very real, and at times zealous. As one resident stated, "Of course we must remember the Southerner likes to hear about the Confederates and their valor and does not appreciate it when we speak of the Southern veteran as a 'rebel.'"[19]

Symbolic was the fate of the Great Peace Memorial. Although the long-anticipated laying of the cornerstone on July 4 failed to transpire, veterans remained undaunted in achieving what was supposed to be the highlight of the Reunion. Two months after the anniversary, Heman Allen traveled to Chattanooga to become a founding member of the Gettysburg Peace Memorial Association, a concerted effort between thirty-four Union and thirty-four Confederate veterans to seek and attain government support. The delegates went as far as to offer a compromise. If Washington could not endorse a marker that showed preference to the absence of war, would they not at least recognize the achievement of the fiftieth anniversary itself? Allen and his colleagues based the request on their motto: "Peace hath her victories no less renowned than war." Ultimately, Congress and the US War Department showed limited interest and refused to fund the project. In response, an editorial in the Louisville *Courier-Journal* lamented, "There are many war monuments, but there are too few peace monuments."[20]

What the government did support was the use of Gettysburg as a training ground. Weeks after the encampment closed, by order of Secretary Garrison, the War Department formed two "experimental" camps for college and university students. One was held at the Presidio in San Francisco, the other at Gettysburg. Proclaiming the Reunion as proof of growing martial spirit, chief of the general staff Maj. Gen. Leonard Wood said the new military training camps "will have a tremendous influence in reviving among the youth of this country, especially the college youth, a proper appreciation of each man's responsibility to the country in time of war." Maj. James Normoyle of the Quartermaster Department said, in his official Reunion report, the grand event "taught the younger generation of Americans to venerate the soldiers of the Civil War, regardless of

At the Gettysburg Reunion, Army War College president Brig. Gen. Hunter Liggett (*left*), secretary of war Lindley Garrison (*center*), and US Army chief of staff Maj. Gen. Leonard Wood (*right*) all made public statements claiming that the well-attended Reunion was proof that US citizens were willing to fight for territorial expansion of the United States. (Courtesy George Grantham Bain Collection, Library of Congress)

the color of their uniforms, far more deeply than they have ever done in the past." The nationalist *Washington Post* promoted the experiment, picturing, "young men, active, alert, and ambitious to learn the war game. . . . The youngsters are the posterity of a reunited North and South." A member of the New York Anniversary Commission, and a veteran officer, added in his report, "Teach the youth of America to believe that patriotism is dearer than life, and there need be no fears for the future safety of our country."[21]

The patriotic fervor evidently produced its desired effect. Student turnout at Gettysburg far exceeded that at the Presidio. For five weeks, over one hundred young men camped upon the hallowed ground along Cemetery Ridge to study and practice battle formations, use of modern weapons, and execution of field tactics.[22] Wood's call for military training in public colleges and high schools of course had its basis in the 1862 Land Grant Act, in which states would receive federal assistance to build educational institutions for the applied sciences—with the stipulation that the schools host soldiering programs. Although the engineering colleges sprouted, their military programs did not. That is until 1913, when Major General Wood, with keen support from Secretary of War Garrison, began actively lobbying college and university presidents to implement combat-readiness education for their male students. This project would become, by 1916, the Reserve Officer Training Corps.[23]

Growing governmental militarism and official rejection of a peace monument did not deter veterans from supporting each other. Many former Confederates returned home from the Reunion with testimonies of good will. D. G. Maggard praised the time he spent with other survivors. "I was surprised at the especially kind treatment we received from the Federals," he told his fellow Texans. B. G. Credle returned to North Carolina and said, "Those Yankees know how to entertain, and they certainly gave us the best they had." Fellow Confederate Al Longnecker agreed: "I even had a better time and was treated better than at any of the reunions of our own." Elijah Bowland of Alabama added, "I hope that the chivalrous South will seize upon the opportunity to repay the hospitable Yanks for their beautiful kindness to us." Richard Wright of the 5th Vermont echoed the sentiment. "It was the greatest celebration I have ever attended. . . . While I was there I met a dozen or more of my old comrades, members of my company, whom I had not seen since the close of the war. I also met several from the Confederate Army against whom I had fought, man to man."[24]

There were other tributes. Later that summer, film footage of the encampment and ceremonies played at theaters from Albany to Yuma. In Philadelphia, members of the "Gettysburg Boy Scouts Service Corps" held reunions of their own several years after the event, as did fellow scouts from Washington, DC. Many veterans' groups saw increased attendance and interest in their functions, including Heman Allen's own GAR post.[25] Allen, Fickas, Waldron, and thousands of others also shared their experiences with their local papers and community groups. Thousands brought back memories and heirlooms for their families. All of them represented a collective survivorship. They were also aware that the Reunion may have been the last great adventure of their lives. As Daniel Lane of North Carolina said, "There must, with most of us, be another meeting over the river very soon."[26]

A grateful Allen was slowing down but still active in his commemo-
rative organizations. Two years after the 1913 Jubilee, his old regiment
was about to celebrate its twenty-seventh annual reunion. As the date
neared, Allen was crossing a street one night near his Burlington, Vermont, home, when he apparently did not notice an oncoming motorist.
The vehicle hit him straight on and came to a halt above him. The impact
broke his right arm, both of his legs, and several of his ribs. After four
hours of intense suffering, Allen died. The following month, the 13th
Vermont held its reunion and paid homage to Allen and eleven other
members who had passed since their last gathering.[27]

William Fickas praised his time at Gettysburg profusely and in turn
thanked all the donors who made it possible for his associates and him
to make their long journey. Years later he moved from Phoenix to the
Los Angeles area, not far from the Sawtelle, California, Disabled Veterans Home where he occasionally stayed years before. His rheumatism
and heart disease eventually worsened, although not enough to prevent
his joining the Sedgwick Post No. 17 of the GAR in Santa Ana, where
he sought the same camaraderie and support he felt at the Reunion. On
April 20, 1914, Fickas died of heart failure at his home in Newport Beach,
California. He was survived by his wife Amelia and their two children. He
chose as his final resting place his longtime adopted home of Phoenix.[28]

Moses Waldron eventually retired from his job as a night watchman in
Carthage, Missouri, living out his days with his wife Fannie at their modest home on 914 West Chestnut Street. Survivors of his 28th Virginia were
few and far between, but his family was growing steadily, including five
children, six grandchildren, and three great-grandchildren. Near midnight on February 7, 1928, just shy of his eighty-fourth birthday, Waldron
climbed into bed, lay on his back, and folded his hands upon his chest.
Minutes later Fannie entered the room and spoke to him. He did not answer. Doctors assessed that he succumbed to heart disease, a malady that
had been eroding his health for some time. He would be buried in Park
Cemetery in Carthage, having never returned to Gettysburg.[29]

Preceding them was H. H. Hodges of Union Hill, Surry County, North
Carolina. Buried under a simple marker in the State Road Primitive
Baptist Cemetery, he embodied the millions who endured the war but
would remain nearly anonymous thereafter, lower in stature than the
famous men who sent him into combat.[30]

By 1918 another war created four million new US veterans. Many of them learned how to operate and engage with new kinds of weapons, including airplanes, air-cooled machine guns, bolt-action rifles, and poisonous gases. As the war escalated, some of their comrades trained upon the hills and valleys of Gettysburg trying to master vehicles known as "tanks." Along with the conflict's other innovations, these rolling fortresses were not quite as decisive as proponents claimed them to be. In time, "Pershing's Crusaders" would have their own reunions, with a great many dead to remember.[31]

At Gettysburg, a monument promoting tranquility did eventually emerge. On July 3, 1938, during the battle's seventy-fifth anniversary, president Franklin Roosevelt dedicated the Eternal Peace Light Memorial upon Oak Hill, with some eighteen hundred Civil War survivors in attendance. Tellingly, careworn farm buildings on the knoll that were present during the battle were demolished to make room for the idealized stone homage. As with other Gettysburg monuments communicating a sense of triumph, the memorial featured young female figures. In this case the relief of two young women served as romanticized metaphors of North and South. Inscribed beneath was the pronouncement of messianic salvation, "Peace Eternal in a United Nation."[32] Once again, observers watched individual Confederates and Federals talking kindly with one another and interpreted these encounters as national rather than intimate events. Political figures were particularly eager to conflate any conversation between two old foes as an everlasting reconciliation between the whole of the North and South. Time and again, commentators insisted that each teary-eyed embrace did not involve aging men addressing anything like firsthand loss or internalized issues. Instead, such scenes were frequently and insistently painted as confirmations of "one nation, one flag."

While most veterans present were not opposed to being praised, virtually none spoke or wrote of martyrdom. Predominantly, they sought not monologue but dialogue. Rather than fixating on death and sacrifice, the overriding theme among them involved survival and empathy. In no uncertain terms, Gettysburg of 1938 demonstrated a fundamental disconnect between what a government stated and what veterans needed.

In 1913, as in 1938, the veterans routinely sought and shared stories of survival more than tales of glory. The Reunion's most bountiful outcome was its ability to successfully combat loneliness. The isolation in which many lived was temporarily yet profoundly absolved by the encounter of thousands who endured similar experiences, and who longed to form new memories through that intrinsic support. Concerning their late-age relationship with their government, the most treasured effect of the Reunion for these soldier-citizens came not from messianic speeches but from the resplendent effort to provide them safe water, fresh food, and basic shelter. On his return to friends and family in Great Bend, Kansas, Jake Miller spoke for many by saying that he most cherished "the order and the care shown the old veterans."[33]

Notes

1. Instructions to veterans attending the 1913 Gettysburg Reunion, *Report of the Rhode Island Fiftieth Anniversary Battle of Gettysburg Commission,* 12.

2. *Report of the Rhode Island Fiftieth Anniversary Battle of Gettysburg Commission,* 12.

3. David Blight famously argues that the reconciliation narrative was a conscientious effort among whites to silence the emancipation story and to counter emerging progressive reforms concerning race relations and the rights of minorities; Blight, *Race and Reunion,* 6–15, 384–90. In many respects, Blight's *Race and Reunion* is an extension of Stuart McConnell's *Glorious Contentment,* wherein McConnell sees white Union veterans pining for a white, nationalist, nostalgic view of a country undergoing rapid socioeconomic change.

John R. Neff and Caroline E. Janney find that the veterans themselves were largely not the ones who advanced the reconciliation theme. Many on the Confederate side of the spectrum maintained Lost Cause mythologies and idolatry of Confederate leadership, while Federals often adopted the position that it was the men in blue who maintained the Union and were major instruments of emancipation; see Neff, *Honoring the Civil War Dead,* 216–20; and Janney, *Remembering the Civil War,* 266–69. Robert Hunt corroborates Janney's findings with his examination of Federal veterans in the Western Theater in *The Good Men Who Won the War.* Barbara A. Gannon further illustrates substantive feelings of Unionist brotherhood and shared sense of victory against slaveocracies in *The Won Cause.* Positioned between the Blight and Neff/Janney schools is M. Keith Harris's article, "Slavery, Emancipation, and the Veterans of the Union Cause." Harris largely adheres to Blight's view that veterans emphasized the virtue and valor narrative, but he contends that former Federals and Confederates vied with each other in defining patriotism. Brian Matthew Jordan argues in *Marching*

Home that the public North and South generally viewed the veteran as an unwelcome reminder of the war's enormous cost and intense anxiety, and the veterans in turn often felt alienated. See also Giesberg, "'To Forget and Forgive'"; Reardon, *Pickett's Charge in History and Memory*, 176–93.

4. *Fiftieth Anniversary of the Battle of Gettysburg*, 175.

5. On martyrdom traditions from Ancient Greece to early Christianity, see Young, *In Procession before the World*, 4–13; Dowbiggin, *A Concise History of Euthanasia*, 7–10; Moss, *Ancient Christian Martyrdom*, 3–10; Edwards, *Death in Ancient Rome*, 19–23. On Protestant sects that adopted and adapted classical and early Christian martyrdom concepts, see Leemans, *More Than a Memory*. Concerning soldier martyrdom veneration during and after the American Civil War, see Wilson, *Patriotic Gore*, xi–xxxii; Wills, *Lincoln at Gettysburg*, 62–74; Kaufman, *The Civil War in American Culture*, 38–54; David W. Blight, "The Origins of Memorial Day in North and South," in Fahs and Waugh, *The Memory of the Civil War in American Culture*, 94–128; Philippe Buc, *Holy War, Martyrdom, and Terror*, 42–52.

6. Vincent, *The Health of the State*, 13.

7. Concerning citations, much of the following involves material from newspaper sources, including those from archive microfilm, newspapers.com, and the National Archive's *Chronicling America* database. This is because the official reports rarely quoted veterans and did not mention their individual experiences (nor do state and national archives contain much material from the attendees themselves). In contrast, the primary means of national awareness and information about the Reunion came from the 150 journalists and photojournalists in and around the Great Encampment during the Jubilee. These reports function as essentially the oral histories of the Reunion. Significantly, data mining the in situ journalism was the very means by which this author discovered that veterans viewed the Reunion in personal rather national terms.

1. PLANNING GLORY

1. Henry Huidekoper's initiation of the Gettysburg Reunion, *Fiftieth Anniversary of the Battle of Gettysburg*, 178; Blake, *Hand Grips*, 71; "Planning to Celebrate Gettysburg's Fiftieth," *Philadelphia Inquirer*, Sept. 13, 1908, 12; "Fiftieth Anniversary Battle," *Gettysburg Compiler*, Sept. 30, 1908, 1.

2. Blake, *Hand Grips*, 8; "Fiftieth Anniversary Battle," 1.

3. For the 1887 and 1906 reunions at Gettysburg, see Frazier, *Reunion of the Blue and Gray*; Reardon, *Pickett's Charge in History and Memory*, 94–107.

4. Capt. John C. Delaney, "Impressions of the Gettysburg Reunion," *Harrisburg Telegraph*, July 11, 1913, 9.

5. "Gettysburg," *Nashville Banner*, July 1, 1913, 6.

6. *Fiftieth Anniversary of the Battle of Gettysburg*, 4.

7. "2,880 Die Each Month," *Washington Herald,* July 4, 1914, 4; "Plan Last Kansas Reunion for 1914," *Elkhart Tri-State News,* Apr. 5, 1913, 4; *Dakota Farmers' Leader,* Jan. 24, 1913, 3; "Gettysburg Veterans Will Leave Tonight for the Battlefield," *Arizona Republic,* June 25, 1913, 1.

8. *Fiftieth Anniversary of the Battle of Gettysburg,* 16.

9. Department of Commerce and Labor Bureau of the Census, Bulletin 109, 25; Center for Disease Control, "Leading Causes of Death, 1900–1998."

10. *Roster of North Carolina Troops in the War between the States, Vol. 2,* 181–83; *Burlington Free Press,* June 7, 1915, 9; "Soldier Who Marched with Pickett Tells of It," *Harrisburg Telegraph,* July 3, 1913, 5; "Veteran Dies," *Carthage Evening Press,* Feb. 8, 1928, 1; "Died by Flame," *Arizona Republic,* Sept. 5, 1901, 1; "Funeral of Mrs. Conger," *Arizona Republic,* Sept. 6, 1901, 1.

11. NARA, Carded Records Showing Military Service of Soldiers Who Fought in Confederate Organizations of North Carolina, Record Group 109, Roll 280. Hodges's 1885 military pension application incorrectly records his enlistment as April 1, 1862: State Archives of North Carolina, Pension Bureau; "Blue and Gray in Great Reunion," *Virginia Gazette,* Feb. 6, 1913, 4.

12. "Happenings of the Past Year," *Gettysburg Times,* Jan. 1, 1913, 1.

13. "Special to Gettysburg," *Salisbury Evening Post,* June 27, 1913, 4; US Department of Labor, Bureau of Labor Statistics; "The Old Soldiers," *Bismarck Tribune,* Jan. 9, 1913, 5.

14. County Clerk's Office, Chittenden County, VT.

15. "The Old Soldiers," *Goodwin's Weekly,* Feb. 8, 1913, 4–5; *Topeka Daily Capital,* Jan. 7, 1913, 3.

16. "Veterans Alike to State," *New York Tribune,* Feb. 16, 1913, 18; "Confederate Veterans Too," *New York Times,* Feb. 16, 1913, 13; Blight, *Race and Reunion,* 6–15, 384–90.

17. *Fiftieth Anniversary of the Battle of Gettysburg,* 36–39; US Department of Labor, Bureau of Labor Statistics.

18. "The Field of Gettysburg," *Democrat and Chronicle,* July 3, 1893, 1; Report of the New York State Commission, 15.

19. Report of the New York State Commission, 14–15; "Fiftieth Anniversary of the Battle," *Harrisburg Telegraph,* Jan. 5, 1915, 13; "The Reunion at Gettysburg," *Times-Democrat,* June 30, 1913, 8.

20. "A Certain Sort of Fame," *Pittsburgh Post-Gazette,* June 29, 1913, 34.

21. "Veterans to Make Choice," *Waco Morning News,* Jan. 25, 1913, 3; Marvel, "The Battle of Saltville: Massacre or Myth?," 10–19; Mays, *The Saltville Massacre,* 46–68; Smith, *Black Soldiers in Blue,* 216–17.

22. "Lively Meeting of Commission," *Gettysburg Times,* Jan. 25, 1913, 1.

23. "Lively Meeting of Commission," 1.

24. "Lively Meeting of Commission," 1; "Veterans to Make Choice," 3.

25. "Veterans to Make Choice," 3.

26. *Fiftieth Anniversary of the Battle of Gettysburg,* 36–39.

27. *Fiftieth Anniversary of the Battle of Gettysburg*, 36–39; "Veteran Dies," 1.

28. *Burlington Free Press*, June 7, 1915, 8; *Indiana at the Fiftieth Anniversary of the Battle of Gettysburg*, 114–21; Hollingsworth, *History of Surry County*, 222; State of North Carolina, *Index to Marriage Bonds*, Surry County, June 7, 1863; "Veteran Dies," 1; "Soldier Who Marched with Pickett Tells of It," 5.

29. "A. P. Hill Camp," *Times Dispatch*, July 12, 1913, 3; "Local Briefs," *High Point Enterprise*, June 20, 1913, 1.

30. *Lansing State Journal*, May 20, 1913, 1; "The Gettysburg Fund Beautifully Growing," *Arizona Republic*, June 21, 1913, 1; "Veterans before Their Departure for Gettysburg," *Houston Post*, June 29, 1913, 48.

31. *Houston Post*, June 26, 1913, 8.

32. "Veterans before Their Departure for Gettysburg," 48.

33. "Great Deeds of the Men of Mississippi Plead for Their Presence at Reunion," *Times-Democrat*, Jan. 26, 1913, 18; "Pulaski," *Times Dispatch*, Apr. 20, 1913, 1; "Vets Gather on Historic Battlefield," *Arkansas Democrat*, June 30, 1913, 1; "Strong in His Praise," *Houston Post*, July 13, 1913, 6.

34. Sturtevant, *Pictorial History*, 437.

35. Sturtevant, *Pictorial History*, 438; *Burlington Free Press*, June 7, 1915, 8–9.

36. "Gettysburg Anniversary Commission," *Burlington Free Press*, Jan. 30, 1913, 8.

37. "Veteran Dies," 1; NARA, Carded Records Showing Military Service of Soldiers Who Fought in Confederate Organizations, Record Group 109, Roll 749; NARA, Carded Records Showing Military Service of Soldiers Who Fought in Confederate Organizations, Record Group 109, Roll 57; "Soldier Who Marched with Pickett Tells of It," 5.

38. NARA Carded Records Showing Military Service of Soldiers Who Fought in Confederate Organizations; "Veteran Dies," 1.

39. "Soldier Who Marched with Pickett Tells of It," 5; "Veteran Dies," 1; George T. Fleming, "Human Interest Stories of Gettysburg Celebration," *Pittsburgh Post-Gazette*, July 5, 1913, 6.

40. NARA, Registers of Enlistments in the United States Army, Record Group 94, Roll 75, 274; NARA, Historical Register of National Homes for Disabled Volunteer Soldiers, Record Group 15, Mf 1749, 6685.

41. "The Gettysburg Fund Beautifully Growing," 1; NARA, Registers of Enlistments in the United States Army, Record Group 15, Roll 718, 274; NARA, Historical Register of National Homes for Disabled Volunteer Soldiers, Record Group 15, Mf 1749, 6685; "Gettysburg Veterans Will Leave Tonight for the Battlefield," 1.

42. NARA, Carded Records Showing Military Service of Soldiers Who Fought in Confederate Organizations of North Carolina, Record Group 109, Roll 280; Jordan, *North Carolina Troops*, 559.

43. State of North Carolina, *Index to Marriage Bonds*, Surry County, June 7, 1863; James J. Farrell, "Old Soldiers Flash Signal of Good Will," *Pittsburgh Press*, July 5, 1913, 1; Jordan, *North Carolina Troops*, 559; NARA, Carded Records Showing Military Service of Soldiers Who Fought in Confederate Organizations

of North Carolina, Record Group 109, Roll 280; United States Census Bureau, Ninth US Census; United States Census Bureau, Thirteenth US Census.

2. GETTING THERE

1. *Report of the Rhode Island Fiftieth Anniversary Battle of Gettysburg Commission*, 12; Bureau of Railway Economics, *Comparative Railway Statistics*, 12.

2. Black, *Railroads of the Confederacy*, 143–45.

3. "Washington Vets Arrive in Akron," *Akron Beacon Journal*, June 30, 1913, 10; "Editorial Correspondence," *Emmons County Record*, July 17, 1913, 4; "Special to Gettysburg," *Salisbury Evening Post*, June 27, 1913, 4.

4. Chester F. Durfeet, Gettysburg National Military Park Library, 50th Reunion, 1913: Participation Accounts, Folder 11–61b; "Washington Vets Arrive in Akron," 10; "Balloted on Route," *Houston Post*, June 28, 1913, 1, 7; "Editorial Correspondence," 4; "Special to Gettysburg," 4; "Great Host at Gettysburg for Celebration," *Belvidere Daily Republican*, June 30, 1913, 6; "Gettysburg Veterans 600 Strong, Depart amid Throng's Cheers," *Detroit Free Press*, June 29, 1913, 2.

5. "Gettysburg Veterans Will Leave Tonight for the Battlefield," *Arizona Republic*, June 25, 1913, 1.

6. "Gettysburg Veterans Will Leave Tonight for the Battlefield," 1.

7. Kenfield, *Vermont at Gettysburg*, 26.

8. *Fiftieth Anniversary of the Battle of Gettysburg*, 189.

9. "Gettysburg Veterans 600 Strong, Depart amid Throng's Cheers," 1–2.

10. *Fiftieth Anniversary of the Battle of Gettysburg*, 196.

11. George T. Fleming, "Human Interest Stories of Gettysburg Celebration," *Pittsburgh Post-Gazette*, July 5, 1913, 6. William Gooley also had his name appear as "Goolidy" in his Confederate records, and he often signed his name "Goolidy" in his officer reports. "Vets Camped Where They Battled," *Mount Carmel Item*, July 1, 1913.

12. "Soldier Who Marched with Pickett Tells of It," *Harrisburg Telegraph*, July 3, 1913, 5; NARA, Organization Index to Pension Files of Veterans Who Served between 1861 and 1900, Record Group 15, 584; NARA, Historical Register of National Homes for Disabled Volunteer Soldiers, Record Group 15, Mf 1749, 6685; NARA, Veterans Administration Pension Payment Cards, 1907–1933, Record Group 15, Roll 724; NARA, Registers of Enlistments in the United States Army, Record Group 15, Rolls 718, 274; Pennsylvania Historical and Museum Commission, Pennsylvania State Death Certificates, Record Group 11; *Indiana at the Fiftieth Anniversary of the Battle of Gettysburg*, 33.

13. Associated Press, "Sixty Babies Die from Heat," *Times Herald*, July 3, 1913, 1.

14. "Many Die from Heat in Chicago," *Arizona Republic*, July 1, 1913, 1; "The Weather," *Pittsburgh Post-Gazette*, June 30, 1913, 2; "The Dead," *Pittsburgh Daily Post*, June 30, 1913, 1.

15. "Veterans before Their Departure for Gettysburg," *Houston Post*, June 29, 1913, 48; "To Attend Old Soldiers' Reunion," *Brazil Daily Times*, June 30, 1913, 6; "Had a Glorious Time," *Houston Post*, July 13, 1913, 7; "Wisconsin Veteran Here," *News Journal*, July 3, 1913, 1; "Colonel Reed Visits Brigham Young Home," *Salt Lake Tribune*, July 23, 1913, 5.

16. *Fiftieth Anniversary of the Battle of Gettysburg*, 56; *Gettysburg Compiler*, July 16, 1913, 6.

17. "Veterans in Camp," *Courier-News*, June 30, 1913, 12; *True Democrat*, July 19, 1913, 4; "Francis Kells," *Brooklyn Daily Eagle*, June 30, 1913, 3.

18. *Fiftieth Anniversary of the Battle of Gettysburg*, 36–37; "Myerstown Men at Gettysburg," *Reading Times*, July 3, 1913, 10.

19. "Have Small Reunion," *Ottumwa Tri-Weekly Courier*, July 1, 1913, 7; "Foemen of Old Meet in Concord 50 Years after Battle," *San Francisco Call*, July 4, 1913, 6; "Civil War Vets Held Rally in English Town," *Asheville Weekly Citizen*, July 31, 1913, 5; "Riddle Veteran," *News-Review*, July 30, 1913, 5.

20. "Gettysburg 50 Years After," *Poughkeepsie Eagle-News*, June 30, 1913, 8; "Gettysburg Service at Baptist Church," *Salt Lake Tribune*, June 30, 1913, 12; "Brave Old Boys of Blue and Gray," *Logan Republican*, July 1, 1913, 8; from "Gettysburg, Past and Present," *Baltimore Sun*, June 30, 1913, 6.

21. "Scouts to Guide Veterans," *Houston Post*, June 26, 1913, 8.

22. "Out of Window," *Adams County News*, July 5, 1913, 6; "Civil War Veterans Hold Reunion," *Pittsburgh Post-Gazette*, Sept. 1, 1915, 5.

23. *Report of the Rhode Island Fiftieth Anniversary Battle of Gettysburg Commission*, 12–13.

24. "Toll Free to Gettysburg," *Gettysburg Compiler*, July 2, 1913, 1.

25. "Gettysburg a Warm Place," *Fort Wayne Daily News*, July 1, 1913, 1.

26. "Washington Vets Arrive in Akron," 10.

27. J. W. Wofford, "Memories of the Civil War Trip to Re-union at Gettysburg," *Western Carolina Democrat*, July 17, 1913, 7.

28. J. T. B. Hoover, Sept. 8, 1913, Gettysburg National Military Park Library, 50th Reunion, 1913: Participation Accounts, Folder 11–61b.

29. "Gettysburg," *Russell Register*, July 25, 1913, 5.

30. "Valuable Information for Old Soldiers," *Greensboro Daily News*, June 27, 1913, 3; "Tar Heel Veteran Drops Dead at Railway Station," *News and Observer*, July 6, 1913, 11; "Great Reunion at Gettysburg Field Practically Ends," *Asheville Citizen-Times*, July 6, 1913, 1.

31. "50,000 Civil War Veterans on Field of Gettysburg," *Evening World*, June 30, 1913, 2.

32. "Valuable Information for Old Soldiers," 3.

33. "Bay State Veterans Charge Grand Central," *New York Tribune*, July 6, 1913, 3.

3. ARRIVAL

1. "25,000 Old Soldiers Arrived Yesterday," *Williamsport Sun-Gazette,* June 30, 1913, 2. A Captain Dalton of the Quartermasters Department said, "The first night (June 28) 17,000 more came than were expected," "Gettysburg a Warm Place," *Fort Wayne Daily News,* July 1, 1913, 1; "Veterans Here by Thousands," *Gettysburg Times,* June 30, 1913, 1.

2. George A. Campsey, "Two Accidents Mar Reunion of Veterans," *Pittsburgh Post-Gazette,* June 30, 1913, 1; "Greatest Spectacle of History," *Philadelphia Inquirer,* July 2, 1913, 1; "50,000 Civil War Veterans on Field of Gettysburg," *Evening World,* June 30, 1913, 2.

3. "50,000 Civil War Veterans on Field of Gettysburg," 2.

4. NARA, Historical Register of National Homes for Disabled Volunteer Soldiers, Record Group 15, Mf 1749, 6685; NARA, Carded Records Showing Military Service of Soldiers Who Fought in Confederate Organizations, Record Group 109, Roll 749; "Soldier Who Marched with Pickett Tells of It," *Harrisburg Telegraph,* July 3, 1913, 5; Jordan, *North Carolina Troops,* 559; "Veterans Organize," *Baltimore Sun,* July 2, 1913, 2; "Oakland Brevities," *San Francisco Call,* June 22, 1913, 68; "Gettysburg Veterans 600 Strong, Depart amid Throng's Cheers," *Detroit Free Press,* June 29, 1913, 2; "Humorous Incidents at Big Encampment," *Evening News,* July 1, 1913, 1; "Men with Empty Sleeves Meet," *Philadelphia Inquirer,* June 30, 1913, 2.

5. "Heat Prostrates Gettysburg Host," *New York Times,* June 30, 1913, 1.

6. "Touching Scenes as Veterans Tour Field," *Philadelphia Inquirer,* June 30, 1913, 2; "Veterans before Their Departure for Gettysburg," *Houston Post,* June 29, 1913, 48; *Salem News,* July 24, 1913, 3.

7. "Advanced Guard of Great Peace Army Is at Gettysburg," *Asheville Citizen-Times,* June 29, 1913, 3; "With Blue and Gray at Gettysburg," *Review,* July 10, 1913, 7; "Army of Peace at Gettysburg," *Wilkes-Barre Record,* June 30, 1913, 16.

8. "Accidents and Deaths in Camp," *Gettysburg Times,* June 30, 1913, 1; 1st Maine Cavalry, Company L, NARA, Organization Index to Pension Files of Veterans Who Served between 1861 and 1900, Record Group 15; W. L. Ormerod, "Blue and Gray United in Camp," *Washington Times,* June 30, 1913, 7; "Death and Injuries at Veterans' Camp," *Pittsburgh Daily Post,* June 30, 1913, 1.

9. "The Gettysburg Reunion," *Town Talk,* June 30, 1913, 8.

10. Charles Gillespie, "Expectations Surpassed by Reunion's Great Size," *Pittsburgh Press,* June 30, 1913, 2.

11. *Report of the Rhode Island Fiftieth Anniversary Battle of Gettysburg Commission,* 11.

12. "Exercises Will Be Short," *Democrat and Chronicle,* June 30, 1913, 1.

13. "Big Army Pouring into Camp," *Pittsburgh Press,* June 29, 1913, 4.

14. "Meadeboro: The Tented Village," pamphlet printed in Syracuse, NY, by Gaylord Bros., 1913, Gettysburg National Military Park Library, 50th Anniversary

and Grand Reunion, Reunion, 1913, Folder 11–61; "50th Anniversary Is Here," *Gettysburg Compiler,* July 2, 1913, 1; "Busy Place," *Gettysburg Times,* July 1, 1913, 1; "A Mushroom City," *Baltimore Sun,* June 29, 1913, 20; "Meadeboro," *Altoona Tribune,* June 6, 1913, 5; "Preparing for Anniversary," *Adams County News,* June 7, 1913, 5.

15. "Fakers Reap Harvest," *Baltimore Sun,* June 29, 1913, 20.

16. "A Mushroom City," 20.

17. Campsey, "Two Accidents Mar Reunion of Veterans," 2.

18. "The Gettysburg Reunion," 8.

19. *State of New York Fiftieth Anniversary of the Battle of Gettysburg,* 24.

20. Blake, *Hand Grips,* 19.

21. Capt. John C. Delaney, "Impressions of the Gettysburg Reunion," *Harrisburg Telegraph,* July 12, 1913, 2.

22. Kenfield, *Vermont at Gettysburg,* 26; *Fiftieth Anniversary of the Battle of Gettysburg,* 40–41, 281.

23. *Fiftieth Anniversary of the Battle of Gettysburg,* 85; McPherson, *Battle Cry of Freedom,* 19–20; Blake, *Hand Grips,* 92.

24. Blake, *Hand Grips,* 16, 69.

25. Ormerod, "Blue and Gray United in Camp," 7; "Weather Unbearable," *Courier-Journal,* June 29, 1913, 1.

26. Gettysburg National Military Park Library, 50th Reunion, 1913: Participation Accounts, Folder 11–61b; "Editorial Correspondence," *Emmons County Record,* July 17, 1913, 4.

27. *Fiftieth Anniversary of the Battle of Gettysburg,* 81.

28. Patterson, *Debris of Battle,* 53–55; Morris and Lane, *Struggle for the Round Tops,* 99. For an examination of what likely transpired at Spangler's Spring, see Archer, *Culp's Hill at Gettysburg,* 136–37n; Pfanz, *Gettysburg,* 377–78.

29. Martin M. Keet, "Gettysburg Camp One of Big Tasks," *Harrisburg Telegraph,* July 5, 1913, 3.

30. *Democrat and Chronicle,* June 30, 1913, 15.

31. Earl Godwin, "Farewells Spoken, Reunion Near End," *Evening Star,* July 4, 1913, 2.

32. Pendergrast, *For God, Country, and Coca-Cola,* 110–15; "Heat Prostrates Gettysburg Host," 1; "Ice Cream Sold Here Condemned," *Gettysburg Times,* July 3, 1913, 1; Godwin, "Farewells Spoken, Reunion Near End," 2.

33. "Blue and Gray Forget Strife on Battlefield," *Pittsburgh Daily Post,* June 30, 1913, 3.

34. "Veterans to Meet on Battlefield," *Angola Herald,* May 28, 1913, 7; *Fiftieth Anniversary of the Battle of Gettysburg,* 81–83; Blake, *Hand Grips,* 19; "Veterans to Meet on Battlefield," 7.

35. Cosmas, *An Army for Empire,* 289–91; "General Miles Blames Powers," *Honolulu Advertiser,* Aug. 14, 1913, 2.

36. Jordan, *North Carolina Troops,* 555–62; Sturtevant, *Pictorial History,* 113, 167, 395, 436, 460, 475, 530, 535, 543, 569–71, 581, 597–99, 607, 618, 652, 680,

700, 705, 716, 728; "State's Health Experts Think Danger Is Grave," *Times Dispatch*, June 24, 1913, 1, 3; "Typhoid at West Reading," *Harrisburg Daily Independent*, July 3, 1913, 2.

37. Baxter, *Gallant Fourteenth*, 80; NARA, Carded Records Showing Military Service of Soldiers Who Fought in Confederate Organizations of North Carolina, Record Group 109, Roll 280.

38. *Fiftieth Anniversary of the Battle of Gettysburg*, 79–81.

39. *Fiftieth Anniversary of the Battle of Gettysburg*, 77–79.

40. *Fiftieth Anniversary of the Battle of Gettysburg*, 53–55.

41. *Fiftieth Anniversary of the Battle of Gettysburg*, 57; Blake, *Hand Grips*, 19; "Feeding Vets at Gettysburg," *Oswego Daily Palladium*, July 17, 1913, in Gettysburg National Military Park Library, File 147th NY Infantry, Oswego County Historical Society File CW 4-4; "Gettysburg Camp Is Real Health Resort," *Pittsburgh Post-Gazette*, July 5, 1913, 6.

4. THE NEED TO FIND

1. Charles Gillespie, "Expectations Surpassed by Reunion's Great Size," *Pittsburgh Press*, June 30, 1913, 2.

2. W. L. Ormerod, "Blue and Gray United in Camp," *Washington Times*, June 30, 1913, 1; *Pittsburgh Post-Gazette*, July 1, 1913, 2; Blake, *Hand Grips*, 106.

3. "Arizona Veterans Are Tenting on Old Battlefield," *Arizona Republic*, July 1, 1913, 1; "Grand Army of the Republic," *Arizona Republic*, Oct. 5, 1913, 12; "Advanced Guard of Great Peace Army Is at Gettysburg," *Asheville Citizen-Times*, June 29, 1913, 3.

4. "Veterans Enroute to Scene of Struggle Half Century Ago," *Arizona Republic*, June 26, 1913, 1; NARA, Carded Records Showing Military Service of Soldiers Who Fought in Confederate Organizations, Record Group 109, Roll 192. Emil Ganz's last name was also spelled "Gantz" and "Gantze" (NARA, Carded Records Showing Military Service of Soldiers Who Fought in Confederate Organizations, Record Group 109, Roll 335). Gottfried, *The Maps of Gettysburg*, 120–29.

5. "Veterans Enroute to Scene of Struggle Half Century Ago," 1; NARA, Carded Records Showing Military Service of Soldiers Who Fought in Confederate Organizations, Record Group 109, Roll 192; NARA, Carded Records Showing Military Service of Soldiers Who Fought in Confederate Organizations, Record Group 109, Roll 335; Gottfried, *The Maps of Gettysburg*, 120–29.

6. "Veterans Enroute to Scene of Struggle Half Century Ago," 1; NARA, Carded Records Showing Military Service of Soldiers Who Fought in Confederate Organizations, Record Group 109, Roll 192; NARA, Carded Records Showing Military Service of Soldiers Who Fought in Confederate Organizations, Record Group 109, Roll 335; Gottfried, *The Maps of Gettysburg*, 120–29; Holzer, *Lincoln and the Power of the Press*, 433–34; Dreese, *Torn Families*, 11–12.

7. "Veterans Saw Former Places," *Arizona Republic*, July 9, 1913, 5.

8. "Fearful Field but Beautiful," *Arizona Republic*, July 22, 7; "First Veteran from Reunion," *Arizona Republic*, July 15, 1913, 7.

9. *Roll of Honor, Vol. XXVII*, 160; *Roll of Honor, Vol. XXIV*, 7; *Roll of Honor, Vol. XV*, 100–101; *Roll of Honor, Vol. XVI*, 145–46, 89–113; *Annual Report of the Adjutant General of the State of New York for the Year 1904*, 750–882; *Roll of Honor, Vol. XVI*, 148, 136.

10. "Veterans' Ranks Thinned by Heat," *Pittston Gazette*, July 3, 1913, 5.

11. For hypotheses on where Lincoln stood during the Gettysburg Address, see Wills, *Lincoln at Gettysburg*, 205–10.

12. Gottfried, *The Maps of Gettysburg*, 217; "Veterans Saw Former Places," 5; *Annual Report of the Adjutant General of the State of New York for the Year 1904*, 841.

13. Gottfried, *The Maps of Gettysburg*, 218.

14. United States Census Bureau, Thirteenth US Census.

15. "He Saw Much of Gettysburg," *Arizona Republic*, July 29, 1913, 7.

16. "He Saw Much of Gettysburg," 7; Gottfried, *The Maps of Gettysburg*, 208.

17. "Veterans Saw Former Places," 5.

18. Lindsay Denison, "55,000 Veterans Suffer in Heat over 100 Degrees on Field of Gettysburg," *New York Daily World*, July 1, 1913, 2; June 30, 1913, Claude G. Leland Collection, MS 2958.5741, New York Historical Society.

19. "Veterans Here but Few Others," *Gettysburg Times*, July 1, 1913, 1; George A. Campsey, "Two Accidents Mar Reunion of Veterans," *Pittsburgh Post-Gazette*, June 30, 1913, 1; Ormerod, "Blue and Gray United in Camp," 7.

20. *Indiana at the Fiftieth Anniversary of the Battle of Gettysburg*, 20.

21. Gettysburg National Military Park Library, 50th Reunion, 1913: Participation Accounts, Folder 11–61b.J.D.; "Had a Glorious Time," *Houston Post*, July 13, 1913, 7; "Meades to Attend," *Pittsburgh Press*, June 30, 1913, 2; "Chester Veteran Pleased with Reunion," *Delaware County Daily Times*, July 8, 1913, 1; "Had a Glorious Time," 7; Gertrude Gordon, "Local Veterans Leave City for Gettysburg," *Pittsburgh Press*, June 30, 1913, 2.

22. Helen D. Longstreet, "As Mrs. Longstreet Sees It," *Baltimore Sun*, July 2, 1913, 2; Kenfield, *Vermont at Gettysburg*, 28.

23. "Woman Lost," *Gettysburg Times*, June 30, 1913, 1; "Ladies Enjoy Gettysburg Stay," *Springfield Missouri Republican*, July 24, 1913, 2; "The Blue and the Gray," *Evening Times-Republican*, July 2, 1913, 4.

24. Evidently common is the phenomenon of postmemory, a.k.a., secondary post-traumatic stress disorder among family members of combat veterans. One event among many researched in depth is the extenuating effects of the Vietnam conflict upon US families; see M. Duncan Stanton and Charles R. Figley, "Treating the Vietnam Veteran within the Family System," in *Stress Disorders among Vietnam Veterans*, Figley, 281–90; Rosenheck and Nathan, "Secondary Traumatization in Children of Vietnam Veterans," 273–88; Terr, "Family Anxiety after Traumatic Events," 15–19.

25. "Woman Lost," 1; "Ladies Enjoy Gettysburg Stay," 2; "The Blue and the Gray," 4. Marianne Hirsch first coined and applied the concept of postmemory in reference to descendants of Holocaust survivors. She later expanded its relevance to individuals or groups affected by the memory and images of others who underwent a life-altering event but did not directly experience the event themselves (Hirsch, *The Generation of Postmemory*). Longstreet, "As Mrs. Longstreet Sees It," 2.

26. "Guns Are Fired on Cemetery Ridge," *Times Dispatch*, July 2, 1913, 2.

27. "Girl at Gettysburg," O*shkosh Daily Northwestern*, July 18, 1913, 14.

28. "Return from Gettysburg," *Denison Review*, July 16, 1913, 1; "Ladies of G.A.R. Urge Pensions to All Vets' Widows," *Des Moines Tribune*, July 10, 1913, 1.

29. Earl Godwin, "Farewells Spoken, Reunion Near End," *Evening Star*, July 4, 1913, 2.

30. Capt. John C. Delaney, "Impressions of the Gettysburg Reunion," *Harrisburg Telegraph*, July 12, 1913, 2. For late nineteenth- and early twentieth-century development of nursing programs in United States higher education, see D'Antonio, *American Nursing*, 1–53; Keeling, Hehman, and Kirchgessner, *History of Professional Nursing in the United States*, 45–98; Judd, Sitzman, and Davis, *A History of American Nursing*, 38–93.

31. Ormerod, "Blue and Gray United in Camp," 7; "See No Kisses in 2013," *Marion County Herald*, June 4, 1913, 2.

32. Coco, *A Strange and Blighted Land—Gettysburg*, 154, 158. While Coco assess the medical exodus immediately after the battle to be nearer 90 percent, Gerald Patterson calculates the evacuation of materiel and personnel to be nearer to 70 percent (Patterson, *Debris of Battle*, 110).

33. "Vets Gather on Historic Battlefield," *Arkansas Democrat*, June 30, 1913, 1; Blake, *Hand Grips*, 85; "Hunting Woman," *Gettysburg Times*, July 1, 1913, 1.

34. Longstreet, "As Mrs. Longstreet Sees It," 2.

35. Longstreet, "As Mrs. Longstreet Sees It," 2; Longstreet, "As Mrs. Longstreet Sees It," July 3, 1913, 2.

36. "To Honor Women," *Gettysburg Times*, July 5, 1913, 1; Jones, *The American Red Cross from Clara Barton to the New Deal*, xx, 141–42.

37. "Vets Advance on Gettysburg," *Indiana Gazette*, June 30, 1913, 2; Denison, "55,000 Veterans Suffer in Heat over 100 Degrees on Field of Gettysburg," 2.

38. "40,000 Veterans Sing War Songs," *Pittsburgh Post-Gazette*, July 1, 1913, 2.

39. "Heat Slays on Field of Gettysburg," *Belvidere Daily Republican*, July 1, 1913, 1.

40. Denison, "55,000 Veterans Suffer in Heat over 100 Degrees on Field of Gettysburg," 2.

41. Denison, "55,000 Veterans Suffer in Heat over 100 Degrees on Field of Gettysburg," 2.

42. "Veteran Treasures Ribbon," *Pittsburgh Post-Gazette*, July 1, 1913, 2.

43. "Wearers of Gray to Bring Flags," *Times Herald*, June 27, 1913, 10; Ormerod, "Blue and Gray United in Camp," 7.

44. "Woman Suffrage Resolution Passed," *Lead Daily Call*, Jan. 15, 1913, 1. For an intriguing individual perspective on the passage of female suffrage for presidential contests in Illinois, see Rousmaniere, *Citizen Teacher*, 123–31.

45. "Woman Suffrage Finds Favor," *Washington Post*, July 5, 1913, 3; *Times*, July 13, 1913, 17.

46. Longstreet, "As Mrs. Longstreet Sees It," July 3, 1913, 2.

47. Blake, *Hand Grips*, 17; Denison, "55,000 Veterans Suffer in Heat over 100 Degrees on Field of Gettysburg," 2.

48. "Grave and Gay Sidelights of the Gettysburg Reunion," *Cincinnati Enquirer*, July 2, 1913, 3.

5. "VETERANS' DAY"

1. "An Incident at Gettysburg," *Burlington Free Press*, July 25, 1913, 8.

2. "Confederates Hold Reunions," *Baltimore Sun*, July 2, 1913, 2; "Reunions on Battlefield," *Gettysburg Times*, July 1, 1913, 1.

3. J. W. Wofford, "Memories of the Civil War Trip to Re-union at Gettysburg," *Western Carolina Democrat*, July 17, 1913, 7.

4. "Greatest Spectacle of History," *Philadelphia Inquirer*, July 2, 1913, 1.

5. "Seeking Graves of Dead Mates," *Daily Republican*, July 2, 1913, 7; "Big Re-union at Gettysburg Joy to Springfield Men," *Springfield Missouri Republican*, July 13, 1913, 15.

6. *Indiana at the Fiftieth Anniversary of the Battle of Gettysburg*, 107, 108.

7. Helen D. Longstreet, "As Mrs. Longstreet Sees It," *Baltimore Sun*, July 3, 1913, 2.

8. Robert J. Lifton, "Understanding the Traumatized Self: Imagery, Symbolization, and Transformation," in *Human Adaptation to Extreme Stress*, Wilson, Harel, and Kahana, 8. There is much scholarship on combat survivor guilt. A telling survey from 1985 indicated that among veterans who had endured heavy combat, nightmares and flashbacks were common in 21 percent of them. Twenty-nine percent expressed survivor guilt. Forty-three percent responded that their experiences were "too painful to think about." Enduring negative memories of service including anxieties persisted in 68 percent. Yet at least 50 percent still held fond memories of part of their tenure, including fond memories of friends. Guilt of survivorship was also frequently high among those who rarely or never experienced military engagements; see Glen H. Elder Jr. and Elizabeth C. Clipp, "Combat Experience. Comradeship, and Psychological Health," in *Human Adaptation to Extreme Stress*, Wilson, Harel, and Kahana, 141–43; Schwartz, *Psychotherapy of the Combat Veteran*; Seedat, "War and Post-Traumatic Stress Disorder," 13–16; Solomon, *Combat Stress Reaction*, 85–94; P. Valent, "Survivor Guilt," in *Stress*, Fink, 373–75.

9. *Pittsburgh Press*, June 30, 1913, 2.

10. George A. Campsey, "Two Accidents Mar Reunion of Veterans," *Pittsburgh Post-Gazette,* June 30, 1913, 2; "Visiting Veteran Tells of Reunion," *El Paso Herald,* July 11, 1913, 12; "Searches for Body of Brother Lost in Brilliant Charge," *Pittsburgh Press,* June 30, 1913, 2.

11. Theodore C. Rose, "Gettysburg as He Saw It," *Star-Gazette,* Aug. 1, 1913, 14.

12. "Veterans Here but Few Others," *Gettysburg Times,* July 1, 1913, 1; "50th Anniversary Is Here," *Gettysburg Compiler,* July 2, 1913, 1; W. L. Ormerod, "G.A.R. Men Are Victims of Heat," *Washington Times,* July 1, 1913, 1; "Gettysburg a Warm Place," *Fort Wayne Daily News,* July 1, 1913, 1.

13. Gettysburg National Military Park Library, 50th Reunion, 1913: Participation Accounts, Folder 11–61b.

14. Gettysburg National Military Park Library, 50th Reunion, 1913: Participation Accounts, Folder 11–61b.

15. "Veterans Had Good Time on Field of Gettysburg," *Oregon Daily Journal,* July 13, 1913, 10.

16. "Old Soldiers Much Interested in the New," *Harrisburg Telegraph,* July 3, 1913, 1.

17. "Visiting Veteran Tells of Reunion," 12; Campsey, "Two Accidents Mar Reunion of Veterans," 2.

18. *Indiana at the Fiftieth Anniversary of the Battle of Gettysburg,* 23; Campsey, "Two Accidents Mar Reunion of Veterans," 2; "Open Headquarters," *Gettysburg Times,* July 1, 1913, 1.

19. "Scouts to Guide Veterans," *Houston Post,* June 26, 1913, 8.

20. "Maryland Astir," *Baltimore Sun,* July 2, 1913, 2.

21. "He Saw Much of Gettysburg," *Arizona Republic,* July 29, 1913, 7. Meyerhoff may also have been referring to William Fickas by the latter's middle name, which was indeed Frank (NARA, Carded Records of Soldiers Who Served in Volunteer Organizations During the Civil War, Indexes, Record Group 94, Roll 23). *Indiana at the Fiftieth Anniversary of the Battle of Gettysburg,* 111; Gottfried, *The Maps of Gettysburg,* 223–25.

22. "Veterans Enroute to Scene of Struggle Half Century Ago," *Arizona Republic,* June 26, 1913, 1; "Fearful Field but Beautiful," *Arizona Republic,* July 22, 7; NARA, Carded Records Showing Military Service of Soldiers Who Fought in Confederate Organizations, Record Group 109, Roll 192.

23. "Reunions on Battlefield," 1; United States War Department, *The War of the Rebellion,* ser. 1, vol. 27, pt. 1, 187, 346; Livermore, *Numbers and Losses in the Civil War in America, 1861–65,* 102–3. For life and death in Civil War prisons, see Hesseltine, *Civil War Prisons;* Speer, *Portals to Hell.*

24. "North Carolina's Duty to Her Honored Dead," *Salisbury Evening Post,* July 18, 1913, 2.

25. Ormerod, "G.A.R. Men Are Victims of Heat," 6.

26. Speer, *Portals to Hell,* 242–44. See also Gray, *The Business of Captivity.* NARA, Carded Records Showing Military Service of Soldiers Who Fought in Con-

federate Organizations, Record Group 109, Roll 335; "Meets Brothers-in-Law for First Time at the Camp," *Harrisburg Telegraph,* July 2, 1913, 3; Speer, *Portals to Hell,* 81–82, 137–38, 182–83; and Hesseltine, *Civil War Prisons,* 48, 178–79.

27. "One Gettysburg Captive," *Evening Herald,* June 30, 1913, 6.

28. NARA, Carded Records Showing Military Service of Soldiers Who Fought in Confederate Organizations, Record Group 109, Roll 749. Moses A. Walrond, Company D, 28th Virginia Infantry, was also listed as "Moses A. Waldron, Company D, 28th Virginia Infantry" (NARA, Carded Records Showing Military Service of Soldiers Who Fought in Confederate Organizations, Record Group 109, Roll 740). NARA, General Index to Compiled Service Records of Confederate Soldiers, Record Group 109, Roll 22. Gooley's name was originally listed as "Gooldy."

29. "Ohio Forces," *Cincinnati Enquirer,* July 2, 1913, 3.

30. Harper, *Pittsburgh of Today,* 966–67; *Fiftieth Anniversary of the Battle of Gettysburg,* 95–96.

31. *Fiftieth Anniversary of the Battle of Gettysburg,* 96.

32. *Fiftieth Anniversary of the Battle of Gettysburg,* 96–97.

33. "Secretary of War Greets Veterans," *Amarillo Daily News,* July 2, 1913, 1.

34. "Secretary of War Greets Veterans," 1.

35. *Fiftieth Anniversary of the Battle of Gettysburg,* 103, 108.

36. "Seeking Graves of Dead Mates," 7.

37. "After Fifty Years," Newtown, Bucks County, July 19, 1913, Gettysburg National Military Park Library, 50th Anniversary and Grand Reunion, Reunion, 1913, Folder 11–61.

38. "Veterans Talk Freely about Feeling Fear," *Harrisburg Telegraph,* July 3, 1913, 5; "Famous Charge Retold," *Baltimore Sun,* July 3, 1913, 2; "Gettysburg May Well Be Proud," *Gettysburg Times,* July 5, 1913, 1.

39. Earl Godwin, "Farewells Spoken, Reunion Near End," *Evening Star,* July 4, 1913, 2; F. E. Ruslander, "Home Thoughts Uppermost in Veterans' Minds," *Pittsburgh Daily Post,* July 4, 1913, 8; "Grave and Gay Sidelights of the Gettysburg Reunion," *Cincinnati Enquirer,* July 2, 1913, 3.

40. Kenfield, *Vermont at Gettysburg,* 27.

41. "Vote Thanks to Post," *Houston Post,* July 13, 1913, 7.

42. *Charlotte Observer,* June 23, 1913, 3; *Washington Post,* June 23, 1913, 4; *Fiftieth Anniversary of the Battle of Gettysburg,* 40–41.

43. "Visiting Veteran Tells of Reunion," 12; "Step Up, Yank, and Pay for That Honey," *Harrisburg Telegraph,* July 2, 1913, 3.

44. "Gettysburg a Warm Place," 1;. Ormerod, "G.A.R. Men Are Victims of Heat," 6.

45. "Return of Missing Flag," *Lincoln County News,* July 8, 1913, 1.

6. "MILITARY DAY"

1. *Report of the Rhode Island Fiftieth Anniversary Battle of Gettysburg Commission*, 14.

2. "55,000 Veterans Defy Great Heat," *New York Tribune*, July 2, 1913, 1; Blake, *Hand Grips*, 21–23; "Weary Veterans Come Back from Gettysburg," *Star Tribune*, July 7, 1913, 1.

3. "Veterans Return from Gettysburg," *Philadelphia Inquirer*, July 7, 1913, 14.

4. Gettysburg National Military Park Library, 50th Reunion, 1913: Participation Accounts, Folder 11–61b.

5. "An Incident at Gettysburg," *Burlington Free Press*, July 25, 1913, 8.

6. "Veterans Like to Be Photographed," *Harrisburg Telegraph*, July 3, 1913, 1.

7. West, *Kodak and the Lens of Nostalgia*, 33–35, 82–85.

8. Gettysburg National Military Park Library, 50th Reunion, 1913: Participation Accounts, Folder 11–61b.

9. "Heart to Heart Talks," *Palladium-Item*, Aug. 21, 1913, 4.

10. "Loving Cup Given," *Pittsburgh Post-Gazette*, July 4, 1913, 17.

11. *Indiana at the Fiftieth Anniversary of the Battle of Gettysburg*, 47; Moss, *Ancient Christian Martyrdom*, 3.

12. George A. Campsey, "Secretary of War Welcomes Veterans to Great Battlefield," *Pittsburgh Post-Gazette*, July 2, 1913, 1.

13. "Gettysburg," *Russell Register*, July 25, 1913, 5; *Washington Post*, June 5, 1913, 3.

14. "Step Up, Yank, and Pay for That Honey," *Harrisburg Telegraph*, July 2, 1913, 3.

15. "Gettysburg Mecca for Local Vets," *Pittsburgh Press*, June 29, 1913, 4; "Pennsylvanians Neglected," *Philadelphia Inquirer*, July 2, 1913, 1; "Gettysburg Mecca for Local Vets," 4; George T. Fleming, "Human Interest Stories of Gettysburg Celebration," *Pittsburgh Post-Gazette*, July 5, 1913, 3; "Famous Charge Retold," *Baltimore Sun*, July 3, 1913, 2.

16. For the use of group engagement of shared memories among veterans, see Erwin Randolph Parson, "The Role of Psychodynamic Group Therapy in the Treatment of the Combat Veteran," in Schwartz, *Psychotherapy of the Combat Veteran*, 153–219.

17. For further descriptions of the "talking cure" in the early twentieth century, see Lichtenberg, *"The Talking Cure,"* ix–x; Chung and Hyland, *History and Philosophy of Psychology*, 193–94.

18. "Storm Breaks on Gettysburg Field," *Morning News*, July 3, 1913, 1.

19. "After Fifty Years," Newtown, Bucks County, July 19, 1913, Gettysburg National Military Park Library, 50th Anniversary and Grand Reunion, Reunion, 1913, Folder 11–61.

20. "Over 40,000 Now in Camp," *Gettysburg Times*, July 1, 1913, 1; "Reunions on Battlefield," *Adams County News*, July 5, 1913, 6.

21. "Pickett's Charge Fifty Years After," *New York Times*, July 4, 1913, 3.

22. Kenfield, *Vermont at Gettysburg*, 28.

23. On information systems in the Great Camp, see Martin M. Keet, "Gettysburg Camp One of Big Tasks," *Harrisburg Telegraph*, July 5, 1913, 3; *Fiftieth Anniversary of the Battle of Gettysburg*, 40–41; "Telegraph at Gettysburg," *Harrisburg Telegraph*, July 3, 1913, 8.

24. The ratio of Union and Confederate soldiers at Gettysburg is based on an estimated total of who served in the war and the total effectives who entered the battle. The former numbers are approximately 2.1 million for the Union and 850,000 for the CSA (McPherson, *Battle Cry of Freedom*, 306–7n). The effectives at Gettysburg are estimated to be slightly over 93,000 for the Army of the Potomac and around 71,700 for the Army of Northern Virginia (Busey and Martin, *Regimental Strengths and Losses at Gettysburg*, 125, 260). "Contributors to Reunion Trip Sanitary Right to Select Guests," *Houston Post*, June 26, 1913, 1; "Those Who Will Go," *Salt Lake Tribune*, June 27, 1913, 2; "Heat Prostrates Gettysburg Host," *New York Times*, June 30, 1913, 1.

25. "First to Return," *Houston Post*, July 13, 1913, 6.

26. Kenfield, *Vermont at Gettysburg*, 27; *Report of the Rhode Island Fiftieth Anniversary Battle of Gettysburg Commission*, 17–23; "One Civil War Vet out of Place at Gettysburg," *Harrisburg Telegraph*, July 1, 1913, 3.

27. "Grave and Gay Sidelights of the Gettysburg Reunion," *Cincinnati Enquirer*, July 2, 1913, 3; "Many Old and Shaky," *Vicksburg Evening Post*, Oct. 16, 1917; Sewell, "Hearing Loss in Union Army Veterans from 1862 to 1920," 2147–53.

28. "An Ex-'Reb' Tells of It," *Evening Herald*, June 30, 1913, 6; "Played a Losing Part," *Evening Herald*, June 30, 1913, 6.

29. Byrd and Clayton, *An American Health Dilemma*, 153; Brown, *Upbuilding Black Durham*, 148; *Harrisburg Telegraph*, July 3, 1913, 9. Barbara Gannon offers a compelling reason why a USCT presence may have gone unreported by black newspapers, positing that many editors protested the event by simply refusing to cover it; see Gannon, *The Won Cause*, 189.

30. "Home from Gettysburg," *Alma Enterprise*, July 18, 1913, 5.

31. Blake, *Hand Grips*, 66–67.

32. "Veterans Beginning to Fly," *Harrisburg Telegraph*, July 2, 1913, 1.

33. "Just So," *Ottumwa Tri-Weekly Courier*, Aug. 9, 1913, 3.

34. Blake, *Hand Grips*, 72.

35. Kenfield, *Vermont at Gettysburg*, 40–51.

36. "Eight Stabbed at Local Hotel," *Adams County News*, July 5, 1913, 1; W. L. Omerod, "Three Badly Hurt in Gettysburg Row," *Washington Times*, July 3, 1913, 4; "Wounded Doing Well," *Baltimore Sun*, July 4, 1913, 2; "Six Civil Suits against Henry," *Gettysburg Times*, July 24, 1913, 1; "Six Civil Suits against Henry," *Adams County News*, July 26, 1913, 1; "7 Men Injured in Fight," *Baltimore Sun*, July 3, 1913, 1.

37. "Charged with Stabbing Eight," *Greeneville News*, July 5, 1913, 1.

38. "Wm. Byrd Henry Cases Closed," *Adams County News*, Nov. 15, 1913, 7.

39. *Fiftieth Anniversary of the Battle of Gettysburg*, 90.

7. "GOVERNORS' DAY"

1. "Famous Charge Retold," *Baltimore Sun*, July 3, 1913, 2; "Blunders Spoil the Rehearsal of Pickett's Charge," *Philadelphia Inquirer*, July 4, 1913, 1–2; F. E. Ruslander, "Home Thoughts Uppermost in Veterans' Minds," *Pittsburgh Daily Post*, July 4, 1913, 8.

2. *Fiftieth Anniversary of the Battle of Gettysburg*, 142; "Kentucky and Indiana Figure in Program," *Cincinnati Enquirer*, July 4, 1913, 2; "Gov. Cox a Favorite," *Pittsburgh Post-Gazette*, July 4, 1913, 17.

3. *Fiftieth Anniversary of the Battle of Gettysburg*, 102.

4. Report of the New York State Commission, 50; *Fiftieth Anniversary of the Battle of Gettysburg*, 96; "Secretary of War Greets Veterans," *Amarillo Daily News*, July 2, 1913, 1.

5. *Fiftieth Anniversary of the Battle of Gettysburg*, 129.

6. Gettysburg National Military Park Library, 50th Reunion, 1913: Participation Accounts, Folder 11–61b.

7. "Blue and Gray Act Pickett's Charge," *New York Tribune*, July 4, 1913, 5.

8. *Fiftieth Anniversary of the Battle of Gettysburg*, 168. The *New York Times* estimated three hundred survivors of Pickett's Division and three hundred of Webb's Philadelphia Brigade present, but all other estimates do not approach such a high number for either unit ("Pickett's Charge Fifty Years After," *New York Times*, July 4, 1913, 3). Walter H. Blake believed there were around 85 Confederate and 150 federal representatives (Blake, *Hand Grips*, 106).

9. Fields, "The 28th Virginia Infantry Regiment," 7; "Blue and Gray Act Pickett's Charge," 1; "Pickett's Charge Fifty Years After," 3; "Blue and Gray Act Pickett's Charge," 5 (incorrectly spelled "Deering"); NARA, Carded Records Showing Military Service of Soldiers Who Fought in Confederate Organizations, Record Group 109, Roll 738.

10. "Blue and Gray Act Pickett's Charge," 1; "Limping Gray Men Once More Charge up Cemetery Ridge," *Atlanta Constitution*, July 4, 1913, 1; "Again Charge Bloody Angle," *Courier-Journal*, July 4, 1913, 1; "Blue and Gray Act Pickett's Charge," 1.

11. "Hotter Fifty Years Ago," *Fort Scott Tribune and Monitor*, July 15, 1913, 6.

12. George T. Fleming, "Human Interest Stories of Gettysburg Celebration," *Pittsburgh Post-Gazette*, July 5, 1913, 6.

13. Fleming, "Human Interest Stories of Gettysburg Celebration," 6.

14. Fleming, "Human Interest Stories of Gettysburg Celebration," 6; Fields, "The 28th Virginia Infantry Regiment," 129; NARA, Carded Records Showing Military Service of Soldiers Who Fought in Confederate Organizations, Record

Group 109, Roll 741; "Blue and Gray Act Pickett's Charge," 5 (incorrectly spelled "Deering"); NARA, Carded Records Showing Military Service of Soldiers Who Fought in Confederate Organizations, Record Group 109, Roll 738.

15. Fields, "The 28th Virginia Infantry Regiment," 181 (Waldron listed as "Walrond").

16. "Soldier Who Charged with Pickett Tells of It," *Harrisburg Telegraph*, July 3, 1913, 5; Fields, "The 28th Virginia Infantry Regiment," 146; NARA, Carded Records Showing Military Service of Soldiers Who Fought in Confederate Organizations, Record Group 109, Roll 744; Gottfried, *The Maps of Gettysburg*, 477; Fields, "The 28th Virginia Infantry Regiment," 57.

17. *Fiftieth Anniversary of the Battle of Gettysburg*, 169.

18. *Fiftieth Anniversary of the Battle of Gettysburg*, 169.

19. *Fiftieth Anniversary of the Battle of Gettysburg*, 169–70.

20. "Society Formed of Pickett's Men," *Times Dispatch*, Feb. 15, 1913, 10; "To Camp with War Time Foes," *Gettysburg Times*, Feb. 20, 1913, 1.

21. "Blue and Gray Act Pickett's Charge," 1; *Fiftieth Anniversary of the Battle of Gettysburg*, 171.

22. Report of the New York State Commission, 11–12.

23. "Limping Gray Men Once More Charge up Cemetery Ridge," 1.

24. "Veterans' Ranks Thinned by Heat," *Pittston Gazette*, July 3, 1913, 5.

25. Fleming, "Human Interest Stories of Gettysburg Celebration," 6.

26. "Pickett's Charge Fifty Years After," 3.

27. Fleming, "Human Interest Stories of Gettysburg Celebration," 6.

28. Fleming, "Human Interest Stories of Gettysburg Celebration," 6; "Veterans Return from Gettysburg," *Philadelphia Inquirer*, July 7, 1913, 14; "Again Charge Bloody Angle," 1.

29. Sturtevant, *Pictorial History*, 437.

30. Jackson, *Dedication of the Statue to Brevet Major-General William Wells*, 96; "First Vermont Cavalry," *Bennington Banner*, June 27, 1913, 1.

31. Jackson, *Dedication of the Statue to Brevet Major-General William Wells*, 103–5.

32. Jackson, *Dedication of the Statue to Brevet Major-General William Wells*, 69; NARA, Organization Index to Pension Files of Veterans Who Served between 1861 and 1900, Record Group 15.

33. NARA, Organization Index to Pension Files of Veterans Who Served between 1861 and 1900, Record Group 15; "Will Come Later," *Gettysburg Times*, Jan. 25, 1913, 1.

34. Daniel Smith Gordon, *Baltimore Sun*, July 28, 1913, 7; *Houston Post*, July 2, 1913, 6.

35. Desjardin, *These Honored Dead*, 154–56.

36. "First Minnesota Men Gather at Monument," *Star Tribune*, July 4, 1913, 1.

37. Theodore C. Rose, "Gettysburg as He Saw It," *Star-Gazette*, Aug. 1, 1913, 14.

38. "Were 'Farthest at Gettysburg,'" *Asheville Gazette-News*, July 1, 1913, 1.

39. Busey and Busey, *Confederate Casualties at Gettysburg*, 1977–78.

40. Hawthorne, *Gettysburg*, 38.

41. Hawthorne, *Gettysburg*, 36.

42. Penn L. Throne, "Friendships Are Cemented," *Harrisburg Daily Independent*, July 3, 1913, 1.

43. "Blunders Spoil the Rehearsal of Pickett's Charge," 1–2; "Special Features of Reunion," *Evening Star*, June 23, 1913, 2; Ruslander, "Home Thoughts Uppermost in Veterans' Minds," 8.

44. *Fiftieth Anniversary of the Battle of Gettysburg*, 172; "Vets Parade and Sing All through the Night," newspaper clippings on the 1913 Reunion, Adams County Historical Society.

45. O. H. Stewart, "District Men in Second 'Charge' of Bloody Angle, *Washington Herald*, July 4, 1913, 1.

46. Ruslander, "Home Thoughts Uppermost in Veterans' Minds," 8.

47. "Special Features of Reunion," 2; "Many See Fireworks," *Gettysburg Times*, July 5, 1913, 2.

48. *State of New York Fiftieth Anniversary of the Battle of Gettysburg*, 12; "Fireworks for the Veterans," *Philadelphia Inquirer*, July 4, 1913, 2; *Fiftieth Anniversary of the Battle of Gettysburg*, 172. On post-traumatic stress disorder, Claire Hilton discovered that World War II veterans could undergo degrees of relapse when exposed to commemoration footage of the conflict, even when viewed fifty years after the person's service (Hilton, "Media Triggers of Posttraumatic Stress Disorder 50 Years after the Second World War," 862–67).

49. "Wise Patriotism," *Pittsburgh Daily Post*, July 4, 1913, 6.

8. "NATIONAL DAY"

1. "Veterans Injured," *Pittsburgh Press*, June 30, 1913, 2; F. E. Ruslander, "Home Thoughts Uppermost in Veterans' Minds," *Pittsburgh Daily Post*, July 4, 1913, 8.

2. *Fiftieth Anniversary of the Battle of Gettysburg*, 173.

3. *Fiftieth Anniversary of the Battle of Gettysburg*, 173; Earl Godwin, "Farewells Spoken, Reunion Near End," *Evening Star*, July 4, 1913, 2; Ruslander, "Home Thoughts Uppermost in Veterans' Minds," 8; "Reunion of Blue and Gray Ended," *Tulsa Daily World*, July 6, 1913, 1

4. Emmerson, *1913*, 155.

5. "The President at Gettysburg," *Durham Morning Herald*, July 5, 1913, 1; Einar Barford, "President Wilson Spends Just Forty-One Minutes in Camp with the Veterans," newspaper clipping collection on the 1913 Reunion, Adams County Historical Society.

6. "Exodus from Gettysburg Under Way," *York Daily*, July 5, 1913, 1; "Gettysburg Camp Ends," *News*, July 5, 1913, 1.

7. *Fiftieth Anniversary of the Battle of Gettysburg*, 174.

8. *Fiftieth Anniversary of the Battle of Gettysburg*, 174.

9. White, *Modern Capitalist Culture*, 108–9; Kershaw, "Copper," 1011; Colby, *New International Yearbook*, 188; United States Department of Commerce, Bureau of the Census, *Cotton Production and Distribution*, 79; Eckes, *The United States and the Global Struggle for Minerals*, 8; Woodruff, *America's Impact on the World*, 120; Smil, *Still the Iron Age*, 47; "Tire Production," *Rubber World*, 668.

10. *Fiftieth Anniversary of the Battle of Gettysburg*, 175.

11. Barford, "President Wilson Spends Just Forty-One Minutes in Camp with the Veterans," Adams County Historical Society.

12. "Bay State Veterans Charge Grand Central," *New York Tribune*, July 6, 1913, 3; "Poses with Blue and Gray," *Indianapolis Star*, July 5, 1913, 2; Barford, "President Wilson Spends Just Forty-One Minutes in Camp with the Veterans," Adams County Historical Society; Capt. John C. Delaney, "Impressions of the Gettysburg Reunion," *Harrisburg Telegraph*, July 12, 1913, 2; A. W. Willey, "Echoes from Gettysburg," *Orleans County Monitor*, Sept. 3, 1913, 1, 3; Jacob W. Cress, July 4, 1913, Gettysburg National Military Park Library, 50th Reunion, 1913: Participation Accounts, Folder 11–61b.

13. "The President at Gettysburg," 1.

14. "The Regular Army Way," *Davenport Weekly Democrat and Leader*, July 17, 1913, 3.

15. James J. Farrell, "Old Soldiers Flash Signal of Good Will," *Pittsburgh Press*, July 5, 1913, 2.

16. Farrell, "Old Soldiers Flash Signal of Good Will," 2.

EPILOGUE

1. "Had Big Time at Gettysburg," *Fairmount News*, July 7, 1913, 1; "Dr. Holt Brings Park Commission a Souvenir from Battlefield of Gettysburg," *Times-Democrat*, July 15, 1913, 5; "Few Veterans Remain," *Gettysburg Times*, July 5, 1913, 1; *Houston Post*, July 13, 1913, 7.

2. "Visiting Veteran Tells of Reunion," *El Paso Herald*, July 11, 1913, 12; "Took Ground Home," *Gettysburg Times*, July 3, 1913, 1; "Pathetic Story of Ninth Veteran's Death," *Harrisburg Telegraph*, July 7, 1913, 3; "Reunion of Blue and Gray Ended," *Tulsa Daily World*, July 6, 1913, 1.

3. Pennsylvania Historical and Museum Commission, Pennsylvania State Death Certificates, Record Group 11; James J. Farrell, "Old Soldiers Flash Signal of Good Will," *Pittsburgh Press*, July 5, 1913, 1; "Pathetic Story of Ninth Veteran's Death," 3.

4. Farrell, "Old Soldiers Flash Signal of Good Will," 2; *Sun*, Aug. 11, 1913, 6.

5. "Gettysburg Veteran Is Strangely Missing," *Indianapolis Star*, July 11, 1913, 3.

6. "Gettysburg Veteran Is Strangely Missing," 3.

7. "Missing Soldier Found a Corpse in Cincinnati," *Star Press*, July 12, 1913, 10; "Old Soldiers [*sic*] Dies from Heat Affects [*sic*]," *Brazil Daily Times*, July 12,

1913, 1; *Indiana at the Fiftieth Anniversary of the Battle of Gettysburg*, 36; "Gettysburg Veteran Is Strangely Missing," 3.

8. "Governor Pays Tribute to Loyalty of Veterans," *Indianapolis Star*, July 23, 1913, 15.

9. "Veteran Killed," *Gettysburg Times*, July 3, 1913, 1; "Veteran Fell from Train and Killed," *Wilmington Dispatch*, July 2, 1913, 1; "John E. Young," *York Daily*, July 8, 1913, 2; "Dies as a Result of Injury Here," *Gettysburg Times*, July 11, 1913, 1; "Gettysburg Veteran Dead," *New York Tribune*, July 6, 1913, 3; "Fired First Shot at Gettysburg Dead," *East Oregonian*, July 10, 1913, 1.

10. "Broods over Gettysburg, Tries to Die," *St. Louis Star and Times*, July 11, 1913, 5. (John Ernst Behne listed as "Ernest Behne"); "Veteran Who Drank Poison Because He Missed the Reunion Dies," *St. Louis Star and Times*, July 13, 1913, 1; NARA, Organization Index to Pension Files of Veterans Who Served between 1861 and 1900, Record Group 15, Roll 509.

11. "Veteran Suicides," *Adams County News*, July 1913, 2; "Gettysburg Veteran Dies," *New York Tribune*, July 3, 1913, 6.

12. Chalmers, *Hooded Americanism*, 167, 170–72, 204; Pegram, *One Hundred Percent American*, 200.

13. *Fiftieth Anniversary of the Battle of Gettysburg*, 175.

14. "Fine Time in Camp," *Washington Post*, July 7, 1913, 3; "Cox at Cambridge for Homecoming," *Times Recorder*, Oct. 2, 1913, 5; "Draws Moral from Gettysburg Reunion," *Philadelphia Inquirer*, July 5, 1913, 3.

15. "1915 Reunion in Richmond Is Opposed by Governor Mann," *Washington Post*, July 6, 1913, 2.

16. "See One Civil War Body," *New York Tribune*, July 23, 1913, 7; J. W. Wofford, "Memories of the Civil War Trip to Re-union at Gettysburg," *Western Carolina Democrat*, July 17, 1913, 7.

17. "Annual Reunion Proposed in Bill," *Times Dispatch*, July 16, 1913, 1.

18. "Them Rebs," *Times Dispatch*, July 23, 1913, 4.

19. "Many Southern Tourists Here," *Adams County News*, Sept. 6, 1913, 5.

20. "From Gettysburg Peace Memorial Association," *Courier-Journal*, Nov. 19, 1913, 10; *Courier-Journal* in *Adams County News*, Oct. 4, 1913, 6.

21. "To Teach the Art of War to Students," *Manchester Democrat*, July 23, 1913, 7; "The Gettysburg Reunion," *Rock Island Argus*, Mar. 28, 1914, 4; Report of the New York State Commission, 53.

22. "College Boys in Gettysburg Camp Train to Become Real Army Officers," *Washington Post*, July 13, 1913, 2.

23. On Maj. Gen. Leonard Wood and the development of the ROTC program in U.S. higher education, see Lane, *Armed Progressive*, 180–83; Chambers, *Oxford Companion to American Military History*, 626.

24. "Enthusiastic over Reunion," *Houston Post*, July 13, 1913, 7; "Returns from Gettysburg," *New Bern Weekly Journal*, July 15, 1913, 1; *Houston Post*, July 13, 1913, 7; Elijah T. Boland, "E. T. Boland's Visit to the Gettysburg Battlefield,"

Brewton Standard, July 10, 1913, 4; "Weary Veterans Come Back from Gettysburg," *Star Tribune*, July 7, 1913, 1.

25. "'The Re-Union at Gettysburg' at the Yuma Theater Tonight," *Yuma Examiner*, Aug. 5, 1913, 1; "Gettysburg Service Corps Holds Reunion," *Philadelphia Inquirer*, Oct. 17, 1915, 3; "Reunion Boy Scouts Unite," *Washington Post*, Dec. 5, 1915, 19; "City News," *Burlington Free Press*, Sept. 8, 1913, 8.

26. "Mr. Lane Writes of Gettysburg," *New Bern Weekly Journal*, July 8, 1913, 1.

27. *Burlington Free Press*, June 7, 1915, 8; "Deaths in Thirteenth Vermont," *Essex County Herald*, July 16, 1915, 3.

28. "Here Are Hero Dead Who Served during the Civil War," *Santa Ana Register*, May 30, 1924, 7; NARA, Registers of Enlistments in the United States Army, Record Group 15, Roll 718, 274; NARA, Veterans Administration Pension Payment Cards, 1907–1933, Record Group 15, Roll 724; NARA, Historical Register of National Homes for Disabled Volunteer Soldiers, Record Group 15, Mf 1749, 6685; "Former Resident of Phoenix Dies at His Home in California," *Arizona Republic*, Apr. 22, 1924, 7.

29. "Soldier Who Marched with Pickett Tells of It," *Harrisburg Telegraph*, July 3, 1913, 5; George T. Fleming, "Human Interest Stories of Gettysburg Celebration," *Pittsburgh Post-Gazette*, July 5, 1913, 6; "Veteran Dies," *Carthage Evening Press*, Feb. 8, 1928, 1.

30. *Fiftieth Anniversary of the Battle of Gettysburg*, 55; "Died at Gettysburg," *Twin-City Sentinel*, July 7, 1913, 8.

31. Keene, *Doughboys, the Great War, and the Remaking of America*, ix.

32. Murray, *On a Great Battlefield*, 35–36.

33. "Snap Shot at Local News," *Great Bend Weekly Tribune*, July 25, 1913, 5.

Bibliography

PRIMARY AND SECONDARY SOURCES

Annual Report of the Adjutant General of the State of New York for the Year 1904, no. 37. Albany, NY: Brandow Printing, 1904.

Archer, John M. *Culp's Hill at Gettysburg*. Gettysburg, PA: Thomas, 2002.

Baxter, Nancy N. *Gallant Fourteenth: The Story of an Indiana Civil War Regiment*. 3rd ed. Carmel: Guild Press of Indiana, 1999.

Black, Robert C., III. *Railroads of the Confederacy*. Chapel Hill: Univ. of North Carolina Press, 1998.

Blake, Walter H. *Hand Grips: The Story of the Great Gettysburg Reunion, July, 1913*. Vineland, NJ: G. E. Smith, 1913.

Blight, David. *Race and Reunion: The Civil War in American Memory*. Cambridge, MA: Belknap Press, 2001.

Brown, Leslie. *Upbuilding Black Durham: Gender, Class, and Black Community Development in the Jim Crow South*. Chapel Hill: Univ. of North Carolina Press, 2008.

Buc, Philippe. *Holy War, Martyrdom, and Terror: Christianity, Martyrdom, and the West*. Philadelphia: Univ. of Pennsylvania Press, 2015.

Bureau of Railway Economics. *Comparative Railway Statistics: United States and Foreign Countries, 1913*. Washington, DC: 1916.

Busey, John W., and Travis W. Busey. *Confederate Casualties at Gettysburg, a Comprehensive Record*. Jefferson, NC: McFarland, 2017.

Busey, John W., and David George Martin. *Regimental Strengths and Losses at Gettysburg*. 4th ed. Highstown, NJ: Longstreet House, 2005.

Byrd, W. Michael, and Linda A. Clayton. *An American Health Dilemma*. Vol. 2, *Race, Medicine, and Health Care in the United States, 1900–2000*. New York: Routledge, 2002.

Center for Disease Control. "Leading Causes of Death, 1900–1998." www.cdc.gov/nchs/data/dvs/lead1900_98.pdf.

Chalmers, David M. *Hooded Americanism: The History of the Ku Klux Klan.* 3rd ed. Durham, NC: Duke Univ. Press, 1987.

Chambers, John W., II, ed. *Oxford Companion to American Military History.* London: Oxford Univ. Press, 1999.

Chung, Man Cheung, and Michael E. Hyland. *History and Philosophy of Psychology.* Chichester, UK: Wiley and Sons, 2012.

Coco, Gregory. *A Strange and Blighted Land—Gettysburg: The Aftermath of Battle.* Gettysburg, PA: Thomas Publications, 1988.

Colby, Frank M., ed. *New International Yearbook: A Compendium of the World's Progress for the Year 1913.* New York: Dodd, Mead, 1914.

Cosmas, Graham A. *An Army for Empire: The United States Army in the Spanish-American War.* College Station: Texas A&M Univ. Press, 2003.

D'Antonio, Patricia. *American Nursing: A History of Knowledge, Authority, and the Meaning of Work.* Baltimore: Johns Hopkins Univ. Press, 2010.

Department of Commerce and Labor Bureau of the Census, Bulletin 109, *Mortality Statistics: 1910.* Washington, DC: Government Printing Office, 1912.

Desjardin, Thomas A. *These Honored Dead: How the Story of Gettysburg Shaped American Memory.* Cambridge, MA: Da Capo Press, 2003.

Dowbiggin, Ian. *A Concise History of Euthanasia: Life, Death, God, and Medicine.* New York: Rowman and Littlefield, 2007.

Dreese, Michael A. *Torn Families: Death and Kinship at the Battle of Gettysburg.* Jefferson, NC: McFarland, 2007.

Eckes, Alfred E., Jr. *The United States and the Global Struggle for Minerals.* Austin: Univ. of Texas Press, 1979.

Edwards, Catharine. *Death in Ancient Rome.* New Haven, CT: Yale Univ. Press, 2007.

Emmerson, Charles. *1913: In Search of the World before the Great War.* New York: PublicAffairs, 2013.

Fahs, Alice, and Joan Waugh, eds. *The Memory of the Civil War in American Culture.* Chapel Hill: Univ. of North Carolina Press, 2004.

Fields, Frank E., Jr. "The 28th Virginia Infantry Regiment." Master's thesis, Virginia Polytechnic Institute and State University.

Fiftieth Anniversary of the Battle of Gettysburg: Report of the Pennsylvania Commission. Harrisburg, PA: n.p., 1913.

Figley, Charles R., ed. *Stress Disorders among Vietnam Veterans: Theory, Research, and Treatment.* New York: Brunner and Mazel, 1978.

Fink, George, ed. *Stress: Concepts, Cognition, Emotion, and Behavior.* London: Academic Press, 2016.

Frazier, John W. *Reunion of the Blue and Gray: Philadelphia Brigade and Pickett's Division.* Philadelphia: Ware Brothers, 1906.

Gannon, Barbara A. *The Won Cause: Black and White Comradeship in the Grand Army of the Republic*. Chapel Hill: Univ. of North Carolina Press, 2011.

Giesburg, Judith Ann. "'To Forget and Forgive': Reconstructing the Nation in the Post–Civil War Classroom." *Civil War History* 52:3 (Sept. 2006): 282–302.

Gottfried, Bradley M. *Brigades of Gettysburg: The Union and Confederate Brigades at the Battle of Gettysburg*. Cambridge, MA: Da Capo Press, 2002.

Gray, Michael P. *The Business of Captivity: Elmira and Its Civil War Prison*. Kent, OH: Kent State Univ. Press, 2001.

Harper, Frank C. *Pittsburgh of Today: Its Resources and People*. Vol. 5. New York: American Historical Society, 1932.

Harris, M. Keith. "Slavery, Emancipation, and the Veterans of the Union Cause: Commemorating Freedom in the Era of Reconciliation, 1885–1915." *Civil War History* 53:3 (Sept. 2007): 264–90.

Hawthorne, Frederick W. *Gettysburg: Stories of Men and Monuments as Told by Battlefield Guides*. Gettysburg, PA: Association of Licensed Battlefield Guides, 1988.

Hesseltine, William B. *Civil War Prisons: A Study in War Psychology*. Columbus: Ohio State Univ. Press, 1930.

Hilton, Claire. "Media Triggers of Posttraumatic Stress Disorder 50 Years after the Second World War." *Journal of Geriatric Psychiatry* 12:8 (Aug. 1997): 862–67.

Hirsch, Marianne. *The Generation of Postmemory: Writing and Visual Culture after the Holocaust*. New York: Columbia Univ. Press, 2012.

Hollingsworth, J. G. *History of Surry County, or Annals of Northwest North Carolina*. N.p.: n.p., 1935.

Holzer, Harold. *Lincoln and the Power of the Press: The War for Public Opinion*. New York: Simon & Schuster, 2015.

Hunt, Robert. *The Good Men Who Won the War: Army of the Cumberland Veterans and Emancipation Memory*. Tuscaloosa: Univ. of Alabama Press, 2010.

Indiana at the Fiftieth Anniversary of the Battle of Gettysburg, Report of the Fiftieth Anniversary Commission of the Battle of Gettysburg, of Indiana. Indianapolis, IN: n.p., 1913.

Jackson, Horatio N. *Dedication of the Statue to Brevet Major-General William Wells and the Officers and Men of the First Regiment Vermont Cavalry on the Battlefield of Gettysburg, July 3, 1913*. N.p.: n.p., 1914.

Janney, Caroline E. *Remembering the Civil War: Reunion and the Limits of Reconciliation*. Chapel Hill: Univ. of North Carolina Press, 2013.

Jones, Marian Moser. *The American Red Cross from Clara Barton to the New Deal*. Baltimore: Johns Hopkins Univ. Press, 2013.

Jordan, Brian Matthew. *Marching Home: Union Veterans and Their Unending Civil War*. New York: Liveright Publishing, 2014.

Jordan, Weymouth T., Jr., comp. *North Carolina Troops, 1861–1865, a Roster*. Vol. 6, *Infantry*. Raleigh: North Carolina Division of Archives and History, 1977.

Judd, Deborah, Kathleen Sitzman, and G. Megan Davis. *A History of American Nursing: Trends and Eras*. Boston: Jones and Bartlett, 2010.

Kaufman, Will. *The Civil War in American Culture*. Edinburgh, UK: Edinburgh Univ. Press, 2006.

Keeling, Arlene W., Michelle C. Hehman, and John C. Kirchgessner. *History of Professional Nursing in the United States: Toward a Culture of Health*. New York: Springer Publishing, 2017.

Keene, Jennifer D. *Doughboys, the Great War, and the Remaking of America*. Baltimore: Johns Hopkins Univ. Press, 2001.

Kenfield, Frank. *Vermont at Gettysburg: July 1863, and Fifty Years Later*. Rutland, VT: Marble City Press, 1914.

Kershaw, John B. C. "Copper: Production and Price Statistics for the Period 1907–1912." *Electrical Review* 62:1 (Jan. 4, 1913): 1011.

Lane, Jack C. *Armed Progressive: General Leonard Wood*. Lincoln: Univ. of Nebraska Press, 2009.

Leemans, Johan, ed. *More Than a Memory: The Discourse of Martyrdom and the Construction of Christian Identity in the History of Christianity*. Leuven, Belgium: Peeters, 2005.

Lichtenberg, Joseph D. *"The Talking Cure": A Descriptive Guide to Psychoanalysis*. New York: Routledge, 2012.

Linenthal, Edward T. *Sacred Ground: Americans and Their Battlefields*. 2nd ed. Champaign: Univ. of Illinois Press, 1993.

Livermore, Thomas L. *Numbers and Losses in the Civil War in America, 1861–65*. Boston: Houghton, Mifflin, 1900.

Marvel, William. "The Battle of Saltville: Massacre or Myth?" *Blue and Gray Magazine* 8 (Aug. 1991): 10–19.

Mays, Thomas D. *The Saltville Massacre*. Abilene, TX: McWhiney Foundation Press, 1998.

McConnell, Stuart. *Glorious Contentment: The Grand Army of the Republic, 1865–1900*. Chapel Hill: Univ. of North Carolina Press, 1992.

McPherson, James M. *Battle Cry of Freedom: The Civil War Era*. New York: Oxford Univ. Press, 1988.

Moss, Candida R. *Ancient Christian Martyrdom: Diverse Practices, Theologies, and Traditions*. New Haven, CT: Yale Univ. Press, 2012.

Murray, Jennifer M. *On a Great Battlefield: The Making, Management, and Memory of Gettysburg National Military Park, 1933–2013*. Knoxville: Univ. of Tennessee Press, 2014.

Neff, John R. *Honoring the Civil War Dead: Commemoration and the Problem of Reconciliation*. Lawrence: Univ. of Kansas Press, 2005.

New York State Commission. *Fiftieth Anniversary Celebration, New York Veterans, Gettysburg 1913*. Albany, NY: J. B. Lyon, 1916.

Patterson, Gerald. *Debris of Battle: The Wounded of Gettysburg*. Mechanicsburg, PA: Stackpole Books, 1997.

Pegram, Thomas P. *One Hundred Percent American: The Rebirth and Decline of the Ku Klux Klan in the 1920s*. Chicago: Ivan R. Dee, 2011.

Pendergrast, Mark. *For God, Country, and Coca-Cola: The Definitive History of the Great American Soft Drink and the Company That Makes It*. 3rd ed. New York: Basic Books, 1913.

Penny, Morris, and J. Gary Lane. *Struggle for the Round Tops: Law's Alabama Brigade at the Battle of Gettysburg, July 2–3, 1863*. Shippensburg, PA: Burd Street Press, 1999.

Pfanz, Harry W. *Gettysburg: Culp's Hill and Cemetery Hill*. Chapel Hill: Univ. of North Carolina Press, 1993.

Reardon, Carol. *Pickett's Charge in History and Memory*. Chapel Hill: Univ. of North Carolina Press, 1997.

Report of the New York State Commission, *Fiftieth Anniversary Celebration, New York Veterans, Gettysburg 1913*. Albany, NY: J. B. Lyon, 1916.

Report of the Rhode Island Fiftieth Anniversary Battle of Gettysburg Commission. Providence: Rhode Island Printing, 1914.

Roll of Honor: Names of Soldiers Who Died in Defence of the American Union Interred in National Cemeteries and Other Burial Places. Washington, DC: Government Printing Office, 1868.

Rosenheck, Robert, and Pramila Nathan. "Secondary Traumatization in Children of Vietnam Veterans." *Hospital and Community Psychiatry* 36:273 (May 1985).

Roster of North Carolina Troops in the War between the States. Vol. 2. Raleigh, NC: Ashe and Gatling, 1882.

Rousmaniere, Kate. *Citizen Teacher: The Life and Leadership of Margaret Haley*. Albany: State Univ. of New York Press, 2005.

Schwartz, Harvey J., ed. *Psychotherapy of the Combat Veteran*. Lancaster, UK: MTP Press, 1984.

Seedat, Soraya. "War and Post-Traumatic Stress Disorder." *South African Journal of Psychology* 12:1 (Mar. 2006): 13–16.

Sewell, Ryan K., et al. "Hearing Loss in Union Army Veterans from 1862 to 1920." *The Laryngoscope* 114 (Dec. 2004): 2147–53.

Smil, Vaclav. *Still the Iron Age: Iron and Steel in the Modern World*. Amsterdam: Elsevier, 2016.

Smith, John David, ed. *Black Soldiers in Blue: African American Troops in the Civil War Era*. Chapel Hill: Univ. of North Carolina Press, 2005.

Soloman, Zahava. *Combat Stress Reaction: The Enduring Toll of War*. New York: Springer Science, 2013.

Speer, Lonnie R. *Portals to Hell: Military Prisons of the Civil War*. Mechanicsburg, PA: Stackpole, 1997.

State of New York Fiftieth Anniversary of the Battle of Gettysburg, 1913. Albany, NY: J. B. Lyon, 1916.

Sturtevant, Ralph O. *Pictorial History, Thirteenth Vermont Regiment Vermont Volunteers, War of 1861–1865*. N.p.: n.p., 1910.

Terr, L. C. "Family Anxiety after Traumatic Events," *Journal of Clinical Psychiatry* 50 (1989): 15–19.

"Tire Production," *Rubber World* 66:1 (Apr. 1, 1922): 668.

United States Census Bureau. Ninth US Census. 1880. Surry County, NC.

———. Thirteenth US Census. 1910. Bryan Township, Surry County, NC.

United States Department of Commerce, Bureau of the Census. *Cotton Production and Distribution, Season of 1917–18.* Washington, DC: Government Printing Office, 1918.

United States Department of Labor, Bureau of Labor Statistics. https://data.bls.gov/cgi-bin/cpicalc.pl

United States War Department. *The War of the Rebellion: A Compilation of the Official Records of the Union and Confederate Armies.* Washington, DC: Government Printing Office, 1880–1901.

Vincent, Jonathan, ed. *The Health of the State: Modern US War Narrative and the American Political Imagination, 1890–1964.* New York: Oxford Univ. Press, 2017.

West, Nancy Martha. *Kodak and the Lens of Nostalgia.* Charlottesville: Univ. of Virginia Press, 2000.

White, Leslie A. *Modern Capitalist Culture.* London: Routledge, 2016.

Wills, Garry. *Lincoln at Gettysburg: The Words That Remade America.* New York: Touchstone, 1992.

Wilson, Edmund. *Patriotic Gore: Studies in the Literature of the American Civil War.* New York: Oxford Univ. Press, 1994.

Wilson, John P., Zev Harel, and Boaz Kahana, eds. *Human Adaptation to Extreme Stress: From the Holocaust to Vietnam.* Cleveland: Cleveland State Univ., 1988.

Woodruff, William. *America's Impact on the World: A Study of the Role of the United States in the World Economy, 1750–1970.* London: MacMillan, 1975.

Young, Robin D. *In Procession before the World: Martyrdom as Public Liturgy in Early Christianity.* Milwaukee, WI: Marquette Univ. Press, 2001.

ARCHIVES

Adams County Historical Society, Gettysburg, PA, Battle of Gettysburg, Anniversaries, 1913 (50th) File 3/1.

County Clerk's Office, Chittenden County, VT.
    Probate Estate Files, Box 52, Files 9059–9076, from 1914–1915.

Gettysburg National Military Park Library, Gettysburg, PA, File 147th NY Infantry, Oswego County Historical Society File CW 4–4 50th Reunion, 1913: Participation Accounts, Folders 11–61 and 11–61b.

Library of Congress, Washington, DC.
    Civil War Photographs.
    George Grantham Bain Collection.

Harris and Ewing Collection.

National Photo Company Collection.

Panoramic Photograph Collection.

National Archives and Records Administration, Washington, DC. (NARA)

Carded Records Showing Military Service of Soldiers Who Fought in Confederate Organizations, compiled 1903–1927, documenting the period 1861–1865.

Carded Records Showing Military Service of Soldiers Who Fought in Confederate Organizations of North Carolina, compiled 1903–1927, documenting the period 1861–1865.

General Index to Compiled Service Records of Confederate Soldiers, compiled 1903–1927.

Historical Register of National Homes for Disabled Volunteer Soldiers, 1866–1938, Records of the Department of Veterans Affairs.

Organization Index to Pension Files of Veterans Who Served between 1861 and 1900

Registers of Enlistments in the United States Army, compiled 1798–1914.

Veterans Administration Pension Payment Cards, 1907–1933.

New-York Historical Society, New York, NY.

Claude G. Leland Collection, MS 2958.5741.

Pennsylvania Historical and Museum Commission, Harrisburg, PA.

Pennsylvania State Death Certificates, 1906–1964, Series 11.90, Pennsylvania Department of Health, Record Group 11, Pennsylvania State Archives, Harrisburg, PA.

RG 25.24, Records of Special Commissions State Archives of North Carolina, Raleigh, NC.

Pension Bureau, Act of 1885 Pension Applications, Office of State Auditor, box 6.139.

State of North Carolina, Raleigh, NC.

Index to Marriage Bonds Filed in the North Carolina State Archives, bond no. 145176

NEWSPAPERS

Adams County News (Gettysburg, PA)

Akron Beacon Journal (Akron, OH)

Alma Enterprise (Alma, KS)

Altoona Tribune (Altoona, PA)

Amarillo Daily News (Amarillo, TX)

Angola Herald (Angola, IN)

Arizona Republic (Phoenix, AZ)

Arkansas Democrat (Little Rock, AR)

Asheville Citizen-Times (Asheville, NC)
Asheville Gazette-News (Asheville, NC)
Asheville Weekly Citizen (Asheville, NC)
Atlanta Constitution (Atlanta, GA)
Baltimore Sun (Baltimore, MD)
Belvidere Daily Republican (Belvidere, IL)
Bennington Banner (Bennington, VT)
Bismarck Tribune (Bismarck, ND)
Brazil Daily Times (Brazil, IN)
Brewton Standard (Brewton, AL)
Brooklyn Daily Eagle (Brooklyn, NY)
Burlington Free Press (Burlington, VT)
Carthage Evening Press (Carthage, MO)
Charlotte Observer (Charlotte, NC)
Cincinnati Enquirer (Cincinnati, OH)
Courier-Journal (Louisville, KY)
Courier-News (Bridgewater, NJ)
Daily Republican (Rushville, IN)
Dakota Farmers' Leader (Canton, SD)
Davenport Weekly Democrat and Leader (Davenport, IA)
Delaware County Daily Times (Chester, PA)
Democrat and Chronicle (Rochester, NY)
Denison Review (Denison, IA)
Des Moines Tribune (Des Moines, IA)
Detroit Free Press (Detroit, MI)
Durham Morning Herald (Durham, NC)
East Oregonian (Pendleton, OR)
Elkhart Tri-State News (Elkhart, KS)
El Paso Herald (El Paso, TX)
Emmons County Record (Williamsport, ND)
Essex County Herald (Guildhall, VT)
Evening Herald Press (Ottawa, KS)
Evening News (Wilkes-Barre, PA)
Evening Star (Washington, DC)
Evening Times-Republican (Marshalltown, IA)
Evening World (New York)
Fairmount News (Fairmount, IN)
Fort Scott Tribune and Monitor (Fort Scott, MO)
Fort Wayne Daily News (Fort Wayne, IN)
Gettysburg Compiler (Gettysburg, PA)
Gettysburg Times (Gettysburg, PA)
Goodwin's Weekly (Salt Lake City, UT)
Great Bend Weekly Tribune (Great Bend, KS)

Greeneville News (Greeneville, NC)
Greensboro Daily News (Greensboro, NC)
Harrisburg Daily Independent (Harrisburg, PA)
Harrisburg Telegraph (Harrisburg PA)
High Point Enterprise (High Point, NC)
Honolulu Advertiser (Honolulu, HI)
Houston Post (Houston, TX)
Indiana Gazette (Indiana, PA)
Indianapolis Star (Indianapolis, IN)
Lansing State Journal (Lansing, MI)
Lead Daily Call (Lead, SD)
Lincoln County News (Lincolnton, NC)
Logan Republican (Logan, UT)
Manchester Democrat (Manchester, IA)
Marion County Herald (Palmyra, MO)
Morning News (Wilmington, DE)
Mount Carmel Item (Mount Carmel, PA)
Nashville Banner (Nashville, TN)
New Bern Weekly Journal (New Bern, NC)
News (Frederick, MD)
News and Observer (Raleigh, NC)
News Journal (Wilmington, DE)
News-Review (Roseburg, OR)
New York Daily World (New York)
New York Times (New York)
New York Tribune (New York)
Oregon Daily Journal (Portland, OR)
Orleans County Monitor (Barton, VT)
Oshkosh Daily Northwestern (Oshkosh, WI)
Ottumwa Tri-Weekly Courier (Ottumwa, IA)
Palladium-Item (Richmond, IN)
Philadelphia Inquirer (Philadelphia, PA)
Pittsburgh Daily Post (Pittsburgh, PA)
Pittsburgh Post-Gazette (Pittsburgh, PA)
Pittsburgh Press (Pittsburgh, PA)
Pittston Gazette (Pittston, PA)
Portsmouth Star (Portsmouth, VA)
Poughkeepsie Eagle-News (Poughkeepsie, NY)
Reading Times (Reading, PA)
Review (High Point, NC)
Rock Island Argus (Rock Island, IL)
Russell Register (Seale, AL)
Salem News (Salem, OH)

Salisbury Evening Post (Salisbury, NC)
Salt Lake Tribune (Salt Lake, UT)
San Francisco Call (San Francisco, CA)
Santa Ana Register (Santa Ana, CA)
Springfield Missouri Republican (Springfield, MO)
Star-Gazette (Elmira, NY)
Star Press (Muncie, IN)
Star Tribune (Minneapolis, MN)
St. Louis Star and Times (St. Louis, MO)
Sun (New York)
Times (Shreveport, LA)
Times-Democrat (New Orleans, LA)
Times Dispatch (Richmond, VA)
Times Herald (Port Huron, MI)
Times Recorder (Zanesville, OH)
Topeka Daily Capital (Topeka, KS)
Town Talk (Alexandria, LA)
True Democrat (Bayou Sara, LA)
Tulsa Daily World (Tulsa, OK)
Twin-City Sentinel (Winston-Salem, NC)
Vicksburg Evening Post (Vicksburg, MS)
Virginia Gazette (Williamsburg, VA)
Waco Morning News (Waco, TX)
Washington Herald (Washington, DC)
Washington Post (Washington, DC)
Washington Times (Washington, DC)
Waterloo Press (Waterloo, IN)
Western Carolina Democrat (Hendersonville, NC)
Wilkes-Barre Record (Wilkes-Barre, PA)
Williamsport Sun-Gazette (Williamsport, PA)
Wilmington Dispatch (Wilmington, NC)
York Daily (York, PA)
Yuma Examiner (Yuma, AZ)

Index

Page numbers in italics refer to illustrations.

www.ingramcontent.com/pod-product-compliance
Lightning Source LLC
Chambersburg PA
CBHW031259090426
42742CB00007B/527